UNIVERSAL RECONCILIATION

A BRIEF SELECTION OF PERTINENT QUOTATIONS

*A selection of quotations by some Christian individuals of repute
who have held to the doctrine of universal reconciliation
and a list of scriptures upon which their beliefs are based*

Compiled, introduced, and with occasional comments by

MICHAEL PHILLIPS

*Doubts are the messengers of the Living One to rouse
the honest heart. They are the first knock at our door of
things that are not yet, but have to be, understood.*
                                        —George MacDonald

UNIVERSAL RECONCILIATION, Third Edition, 2013
First edition privately printed, 1998

Introduction copyright © 1998 by Michael Phillips
William Barclay, A Spiritual Autobiography © 1975 by William B. Eerdmans
Publishing Company

Third Edition published by Yellowood House, an imprint of Sunrise Books

ISBN 9780940652170

MICHAEL PHILLIPS IS THE AUTHOR OF...

The Commands
Bold Thinking Christianity
Angels Watching Over Me
A Perilous Proposal
Heather Song
Hell and Beyond
The Treasure of the Celtic Triangle
George MacDonald, Scotland's Beloved Storyteller
Make Me Like Jesus
The Eleventh Hour
A Rose Remembered
Dream of Freedom
Dream of Life
Dream of Love
George MacDonald and the Late Great Hell Debate
Rift in Time
Hidden in Time
God A Good Father
Jesus An Obedient Son

Contents

INTRODUCTORY COMMENTS AND OBSERVATIONS

by
Michael Phillips

My work with George MacDonald through the years has resulted in many individuals seeking me out in hopes that I will be able to shed light on MacDonald's view of the afterlife, as well as clarify for them the subject of universal reconciliation as a whole.

What I have generally tried to do is point such individuals to various passages in MacDonald's own writing, and toward what other sources I feel might be helpful. My intent has been that they read what others have had to say on the matter, and decide for themselves what conclusions to draw.

Raised in the tradition of conservative evangelicalism, for most of my life I haven't known what to make of universal reconciliation either. I have been a seeker along the same road as most of those who contact me. Even now I do not hesitate to say that my own perspectives remain growing and incomplete. What I am comfortable saying with absolute certainty on the matter is this:

I believe that the love, goodness, forgiveness, and trustworthiness of the Father of Jesus Christ are infinite. Therefore, I trust HIM completely. Though he slay me, yet will I trust him, and so may all creation likewise trust him. He is a GOOD Father, so all he does **must** be good and can only be good. His essential nature is LOVE, so everything that proceeds out of his divine will must reflect that love. It is in his heart to FORGIVE infinitely. Jesus told us so. Therefore...we may TRUST him, and trusting him, may trust him for ALL things, for ALL men, for ALL possibilities. What is in the heart of God the Father to do will be full of love, full of goodness, and full of forgiveness. And in those foundational truths of his essential nature and character I rest. In those foundational truths of his essential nature and character are all my questions swallowed up. I am at peace...for I TRUST Him.

Beyond that, I care not to go. I am fascinated and intrigued to explore beyond the boundaries of traditional thought concerning what might be in God's heart to accomplish. But I find no need within myself to formulate a "systematic theology," as it were, of his reconciliatory purposes. I trust *God* far more than I trust in *my* capacity to understand the infinity of his loving purpose.

To speak bluntly, in my view the key reason why those on both sides of this issue struggle so hard to systematize their personal theologies (and err in the process) is this— they don't trust *God* enough. So they feel they must put together a system of belief on the afterlife constructed out of their own incomplete intellects in which they *can* trust.

Something about it, however, seems backwards to me. I would far rather trust God for biblical uncertainties, than to convince myself that I am certain of his will on every thorny issue as many seem to consider it their duty to do. Being wrong does not frighten me nearly so much as being unable to trust God to do what is right and good, though my fallible human intellect will of a certainty be unable to discern how he will accomplish that in every instance.

Having said that, however, obviously I would not make available the result of my own reading and research into this matter, if I did not think the Scriptures pointed to principles which the Spirit of God wants to reveal to his people.

In spite of a posture of open-minded neutrality which I try to maintain on this scriptural conundrum, I *do* believe there are great truths here God desires us to lay hold of. But not so that we may formulate ironclad belief systems which we grow to worship more than the God they describe, but *so that we will know who God is and that our capacity deepens to trust him.*

That is the purpose of this booklet—that all who read it might better know God, not to establish evidences for a belief system.

It is not intended as an apologetic for or against any point of view. I have no desire to *argue* on behalf of or against this or any doctrine. Scriptural viewpoints on contested subjects are interesting to me because I relish in the exchange of *ideas.* But they are not things of the first rank. I would rather expend my energies seeking more deeply to understand the character of God and obeying him, than attempting to determine rightness or wrongness about every debated issue where the Bible leaves room for varying interpretation. Doctrinal "ideas" are something like a hobby to me. They do not form the foundation for my *life.*

The endless jot-and-tittle debate between Christians, it seems to me, has done more to impede the coming of the kingdom of God with power than all the unbelief in the history of the world. I will not knowingly contribute to it further. I will attempt to offer the searching heart direction, as others have offered it to me through the years. But argument is not the aim of this booklet, and I respectfully request that nothing herein be used for that purpose. These are high matters to be discussed with our Father in heaven, to the center of whose heart all questions and controversies and unanswerables must lead in the end.

Prayers, heart-cries, tears, with here and there a little fear and trembling, may accompany the wrestling through of the ideas and passages on these pages. But it will grieve me if brothers and sisters use any of this to line up on opposite sides of this particular doctrinal fence and begin tossing various viewpoints and proof-texts back and forth. Jesus did not offer himself on the cross so that we could be at each other's throats over who is or is not included in that atonement, but that the world might be saved.

On all matters doctrinal, my own points of view are still forming. As I have read and studied over the years, the matter of universal reconciliation intrigues me wonderfully. As I said, I think there may be truth here that most in evangelicalism have overlooked — truth based on who God is.

What follows is a non-exhaustive compilation of quotes and a brief list of scripture verses which indicate a greater reach to God's salvation than is commonly believed. These are passages I have personally found helpful in navigating the maze of opinion and argument to which many discussions of universal reconciliation sadly arrive in the end.

I became intrigued by possibilities outside the orthodox belief system of my upbringing even before discovering George MacDonald's writing. MacDonald furthered the process, not because in him I discovered universal reconciliation as such, but because he forced wide within me new doorways into the inexhaustibility of God's goodness. MacDonald, in fact, persistently refused to articulate a firm position. Yet when one reads his works, one cannot help being stretched into wondrously enlarging realms in the understanding of God's character. While not addressing the controversy of universal reconciliation head on, MacDonald constantly stretches his readers in their capacity to trust in the infinite goodness of God's Fatherhood.

I found the idea by no means fearsome that God might have more in mind to ultimately accomplish in his creation than is commonly taught, but rather an exciting one to prayerfully consider. To my astonishment, however, I was to learn, as do most who explore this less-traveled pathway through the spiritual yellow wood, that those *not* inclined similarly to inquire how expansive might be the love of the God they say they worship, do not find this quest into God's heart exciting in the least, but rather heretical.

Actually, for me this is no mere doctrinal matter. I would not compile a booklet such as this on most contested points of faith. I have never done so before. This issue is different. It strikes at the very core of the Christian belief system—to what extent are God's love, goodness, and forgiveness infinite? Will God's victory in the universe be complete...absolute...total? Or will the devil ultimately prevent God's perfect and complete will (2 Peter 3:9) from being accomplished?

These are very significant questions. Who *is* the God we worship and seek to obey? Is the universe a great dualism, where the two sides of Good and Evil each lay *eternal* claim to the souls in their camp?

Such implications make this an important and vital inquiry. I'm not sure we can truly know who God the Father is in our hearts unless we resolve it. Nor do I think, as F.D. Maurice points out in his essay which follows, that the world has much reason to listen to the gospel until we truly apprehend the character of the God that gospel is purported to be about. Is it truly *good* news we proclaim to the world, while at the same time we speak of the eternal retribution of God against a huge portion of his created universe?

This will make it clear that, though I say that I am at peace merely trusting in the infinite trustworthiness of the Father, I yet believe this is a matter we need to explore. And I have explored it in some depth and am the richer in my walk with the Lord for it.

Those who would not wade into such theological waters often dismiss these questions with a light and subtly pietistic air: "Ah, but brother...you're adding to the Word of God...you must just take the inspired Word for what it says."

Unfortunately, it's not that easy. Much in the Word of God doesn't actually support the orthodox position to the extent its proponents assume. It is precisely the desire to take the Word of God for what it says that first led me down this road less traveled, as is the case with many thousands like me.

Jesus said as clearly as he could (John 12:32) that his death would draw *all* men to him. It's there in black and white, in nearly every translation from the King James (*all*) to Living (*everyone*).

Paul emphasized the same truth when he wrote to the Corinthians (1 Cor. 15:22), "For as in Adam all die, so in Christ *all* will be made alive."

There's that troublesome word **all** again. What do we do with such statements—especially, coming as they do, from the lips of Jesus and Paul?

While we mustn't add to the Word of God, it seems we are under a similar injunction not to subtract from it, and change that *all* to "some" in order to shrink what Jesus and Paul actually said to fit traditional orthodoxy.

For a reason which has puzzled me as long as I can remember, it seems that the multitude of evangelical Christians don't want God to be *too* good. They are inexplicably threatened by the thought that God might be *more* loving and *more* forgiving than they are. This remains a baffling mystery to me. Nor is it a question most people want to be challenged with. It seems they just do not want to think about it.

But as God's people, we *must* think about it.

Do we want to know who God is? Or are we content with an image of him that has been passed down to us through recent years which *may* not even be based on Scripture?

It is a vital query, upon which I have the feeling the future effectiveness of our evangelism depends. If we don't know whether God's love and forgiveness are *really* infinite, what then is the "good news" we proclaim to the world? Merely that he saves us from hell? That with his right hand of love he rescues us from his left hand of vengeance? That the loving Son protects us from the wrathful Father?

That may be "news." I'm not sure whether it's very *good* news.

The people in today's world are more sophisticated than we give them credit for being. This doctrine which puts something like a divine schizophrenia at the heart of the Godhead sounds less than ridiculous to them. Is it any wonder the large percentage of thinking men and women aren't listening with a great deal of attentiveness to this thing that we continue to insist is *good news*?

Do I speak irreverently? I don't think so. Might it not be time we realistically face how the God that we insist loves them actually appears to a large percentage of people? We have to be pragmatic about that fact. We flatter ourselves with minuscule pockets of revival, but the stark fact is for the most part, the world isn't heeding the gospel message. I think it is largely because *we* are confused about who God is and what is his intrinsic character.

It behooves us, therefore, to take a closer look at the implications of universal reconciliation. That is best how I can characterize my own position—I have been engaged in a thirty year process of taking a closer look. I continue to study, to read...mostly to pray, asking the Holy Spirit to illumine truth into my heart, mind, and spirit.

In that quest, the authors included in this booklet are ones whose ideas have helped me and given me much to think about in fresh ways.

One point of misunderstanding must be cleared away

at the outset—a belief in universal reconciliation is *not* "heresy." Numerous Bible believing, sound thinking, men and women of God have held to the doctrine of universal reconciliation throughout the entire history of the church.

This is not to say it is not a controversial matter. Surely it is. However, universal reconciliation is not by definition a spurious nor obviously unbiblical doctrine, such as gnosticism, which sprang up in the first century and which many Christian leaders had to warn against. Respected leaders of the Church have believed in universal reconciliation. The reason they believed it may startle you: It was their conviction (on the basis of John 12:32 and 1 Cor. 15:22) that Jesus and Paul both taught it.

Though it is not recognized in most evangelical circles today, scriptural evidence exists on both sides of what, as I say, we must recognize as a matter of great controversy. Once a man or woman begins opening his or her eyes to the broader view to which many scriptures point, he or she often becomes astounded at what they suddenly begin seeing on almost every page of the Bible. I make that statement, not in an attempt to argue on behalf of the broader view, so to speak, but merely to level the scriptural playing field.

It's not as easy a matter as saying, "I just take the Bible at literal face value." The words themselves (the "words" given us by the translators) sometimes point in opposite directions, as Matthew 25:46 and Philippians 2:10 clearly evidence. Here sit the most obvious proof-texts for the two opposing viewpoints on the eternal destiny of sinners—the one, as translated, speaking of "eternal punishment," the other declaring that "every knee" will ultimately bow in profession of faith.

That's why the playing field must be leveled. The searching heart must come to this question with an open and prayerful mind. The Scriptures simply aren't as clear on the matter as we might wish. Much prayer and the illumination of the Holy Spirit are required.

As it is not an intrinsically heretical idea, neither is universal reconciliation a *new* doctrine. It is as old as the church itself, and has been a respected position to maintain. As the centuries passed, however, on the one end of the theologic spectrum, to the great detriment of the fabric of the church, it gradually has come to be considered heresy. That twisting of a viable scriptural position into a doctrine people are taught to fear has rendered impotent the vital inquiry into the character of God, and thus has seriously weakened evangelicalism itself.

Here we will document some of the writers and thinkers through the centuries, whose study of the Scriptures has led them to the conclusion that God's victory will indeed be complete. It is, of course, possible to compile quotations a mile long to validate *any* belief in *any* position. Men and women throughout history have believed most things it is possible to believe. Enough research can generate "a cloud of witnesses" in support of any doctrine, spiritual or otherwise.

But the following observation might be worthy of consideration. Oftentimes (certainly not every time), *opinion* and a *pre-formed viewpoint* lead the way on the part of those advocating what perhaps would be called the orthodox fundamental position—the view of an endless hell whose purpose is retributive rather than remedial, in which death represents the final and absolute closing of the door of opportunity of further redemption. Writings in support of this widely-held orthodoxy generally (I do not say all) reflect a desire to maintain this already established position. Rarely do you find accounts of "personal search" leading the way into increasingly deeper understanding of this evangelical orthodoxy. In my own experience, I have not encountered the writings of the individuals holding this perspective looking for *more* of God's truth, hungering for a *deeper* reach of God's love, crying out to discover a *wider* extent of God's salvation.

This is a *most* significant point.

In general, Scripture indicates that personal hunger and a search for truth lead to wisdom and understanding, while an adherence to the traditions of men, without a heart-hunger accompanying it, can lead to spiritual stagnation.

A hundred biblical passages could be brought in to support this principle, that *understanding and wisdom come as a result of an intense search for truth* with one's whole heart. The entire book of Proverbs and most of Jesus' teachings and Paul's epistles resound with the cry to leave no stone unturned...to search, knock, dig, seek, pray. Personal *hunger* offers a necessary searchlight into constantly new and deeper dimensions of faith.

"If you *call out* for insight and *cry aloud* for understanding, and if you *look for it* as for silver and *search for it* as for hidden treasure, then you will understand...and find the knowledge of God." (Proverbs 2: 3-5)

How do we imagine that Jesus grew into such confidence and boldness as our Savior that he walked through the grainfields on the Sabbath, breaking the law in plain view of the Pharisees? How else other than by challenging the orthodoxy of his day in just this seeking, searching, praying manner. What was he doing in the temple among the teachers and elders when he was twelve—*questioning* the stale and unscriptural orthodoxy of the day.

The related principle is equally supported scripturally: Steadfastly adhering to a spiritual orthodoxy (*any* spiritual orthodoxy), calling those who disagree heretics, and directing one's study and energies exclusively to the bolstering of that orthodoxy with greater strength than toward the discovery of new and deeper truths...such is a potential pathway toward spiritual stagnation and eventual error. Such does not *always* occur, but the potential danger is always there. Stagnation is a clear scriptural principle—it usually infiltrates status-quo faith.

These two factors, on the face of them, recommend the conclusions of those who have labored in prayer and study over some matter to a greater extent than the conclusions of those whose views are set in concrete on the basis of traditions which often they have not wrestled through for themselves.

This tells nothing *for certain*. A searching individual *may* just as well wind up following a pathway toward error, to which the growth of the cults attests. The perennial "seeker" who makes little headway in life, may be just a spiritual nomad without much of a clue to what's going on about anything. On the other side of it, many traditional doctrines and opinions *are* indeed true, and become widely held just because they are *accurate* interpretations of the Bible.

In what follows, therefore, you have to make some determinations concerning the character and spiritual integrity of those whose words you are reading.

Hannah Hurnard, for example, recounts her personal and prayerful search in detail. Martin Luther's and George MacDonald's struggles to find truth in the midst of the prevailing traditions of their times are well documented. William Barclay spent a lifetime of Scriptural study, gradually developing the view of the afterlife that he did not make public until three years before his death.

Are Hannah Hurnard's and George MacDonald's "searches" prompted by hearts truly listening to God, or are these individuals desert nomads whose experience really doesn't tell us much? And in my own case, does my admitting that "I have been a seeker along the same road myself" and that "my own points of view are still forming" recommend me as reliable witness to these matters, or as a kook who has been out in the desert too long and has had too much sun? These are questions you have to determine on the basis of what you know about anyone you choose to listen to and whose perspective you choose to heed.

Opinion and *tradition* come more into the various arguments in support of so-called orthodoxy, while *prayer* enters more into the personal accounts of those seeking for truth no matter where the search might lead. And prayer, if it comes from the heart of a sincerely God-hungry individual, must yield a harvest of truth in the end. Its compass is pointed in only one direction—toward God. The compass of opinion and tradition, however, can point to any of the 360 degrees of a circle—*toward* truth or *away* from it.

As I have observed this principle at work, there is another factor that reveals itself very differently on the two sides of this doctrinal fence—*open-mindedness.* I witness what seems a deeper open-mindedness toward Scripture on the part of those hungry searching individuals than I have seen from those, many renowned theologians among them, whose aim is to prop up and support the orthodox traditions which have been passed down to them. Now open-mindedness is not in and of itself necessarily always a virtue. Yet it *is* often a requisite to clear thinking. If Peter had not been open-minded on the rooftop in Joppa, where would we all be now? If Paul had not been open-minded on the road to Damascus, where would we all be now? God had to jolt both Peter and Paul out of their comfortable, existing orthodoxies. So open-mindedness can be a vital doorway into truth when God speaks something new to his people.

The difference between this reliance on tradition, orthodoxy, and opinion on the one side, and personal, open-minded search, led by hunger and prayer, on the other tends toward the following result—that "orthodox-tradition" driven studies are more proof-text oriented, while "search-and-prayer" inquiries probe more persistently into the long-range, general, and more overarching purposes of Scripture. On top of this, I have also discovered a much weightier level of scholarship, and more thorough inquiry into the historic meanings of the original Greek texts, on the parts of those willing to look beyond the boundaries of orthodoxy. The scholarship of the studies by Jukes, Allin, and Symonds profoundly surpasses anything I have found by the contemporary "theologians" and authors who are writing on these topics.

Proof-text spirituality was precisely the pit into which the Pharisees had fallen. This, therefore, concerns me about the many studies I have read in support of our contemporary evangelical traditions.

Opinion and proof-text motivated treatises simply do not, in my experience, yield the quality of ore as do those penned by men and women who have struggled, prayed, and searched their way deeply into the mine-shafts of God's Word, led by hunger after God's heart rather than a desire to bolster existing theologies. It therefore becomes a matter of the most serious import in reading what follows, not so much that a list of quotes has been compiled, but that you ask to whom you are listening.

My own pursuit has involved a great deal of reading on both sides of the fence. I have read today's leading evangelical theologians on this matter, searching for truth just as avidly in their writings as I have in MacDonald and some of the others in this booklet. I have genuinely, and I hope humbly, sought to be open-minded and to examine evidence presented by theologians across the spectrum. When fundamentalist theologians engage on discussion at this point, however, I have found their analyses more often than not attempts merely to argue on behalf of the orthodox status quo with automatic knee-jerk scriptural interpretations. I do not find them upturning new scriptural soil, wide-eyed and enthusiastic to see what they might discover. Passages such as John 1:7 and John 12:32 and Philippians 2:10 are dismissed with a wave of the hand. I do not say such personal quests do not exist in fundamentalist orthodoxy, only that I have not found them insofar as this particular issue is concerned. I say this without reproach, only that it is something I have observed.

This difficulty of not being able to find the "personal search" more widely represented in fundamentalist orthodoxy makes the quest all the more difficult. Personally I would very much like to read such an account. But the scarcity of such seems to be a result of the fact that many preachers, teachers, and would-be theologians do not set themselves to prayerfully study the scriptural possibilities concerning the afterlife, so much as they set themselves simply to expound upon what has been expounded by thousands before them.

Dr. Loyal Hurley, before his personal quest for truth began, describes such a mentality. "Like Paul of old," he writes concerning the possibility of universal reconciliation, "I had thought that I ought to do many things against this heretical teaching—everything but to study it!" [1]

Sadly as a result, through the centuries a great deal of superficiality has come to pass for sound doctrine. Anyone may "expound" on any passage of Scripture he likes. If he is a clever writer, he can easily make his expositions and proof-texts and opinions *sound* as if they occupy a level of stature equal to that from the pen of one who has studied and prayed the same matter through for fifty years. But the difference in weight, integrity, and erudition of such expositions is enormous.

Not long ago I perused the shelves of our own Christian bookstore to see what current teachings on the subject of hell were being published. One was written by a former sports figure, a very well known and popular author and speaker, full of attempted humor, cute witticisms, and a general tone which made light of a very serious matter.

---

[1] D. Loyal Hurley, *The Outcome Of Infinite Grace*, p. 1, original publisher and date unknown.

Grievously, the following kind of thing passes for sound teaching in today's church. I quote from his "commentary" on Luke 16:19-21. Lazarus is renamed Larry:

> *"There was a rich kid who dressed well. Clean! Slick! Very together...He lived it up daily. In other words, he was a total party animal...*
>
> *Bill had it all...The best CD and DAT recorder...a forty-two inch tube TV...Of course he was great looking and was one of those unusual teenagers who didn't have any zits...a standout jock; the star quarterback...the top track guy...The luscious lover was great in the girl department...What can I say? The guy was a stallion, Sir Studly....*
>
> *The son of the gardener was named Larry. He lived by the entry to the estate in the gatekeeper's cottage down below the rich kid's house. Larry had a pretty tough life. He had some terrible zits and was covered with sores. We're not just talking simple pimples here. Larry had acne vulgarus. His was a severe case...The medical plan for Larry was obviously deficient, because instead of a prescription for his face...they got a dog to lick his zits...How gross! Poor Larry. (Remember, I didn't write this stuff. You'll have to take this one up with God.)...*
>
> *It came about that this poor, pitiful, and pathetic person died and went to heaven. I think the doctor diagnosed Larry's cause of death as a case of infected zits.*
>
> *The very next day Dollar Bill was driving his 'vette, wrapped it around a tree, was killed, and went to Hades. Looking up, the rich kid saw Larry in the penthouse."* [2]

---

[2] I apologize that I no longer have the reference for this book. It has been so long since I made note of the quote, not intending to use it in a published edition of this book, that I do not remember either the title nor the author.

It is pointless to continue. And painful, to see the important things of God written about in such a careless, juvenile manner. However, this is the sad state to which much current evangelical teaching has degenerated. Many books of this caliber find their way onto the best-seller lists every month.

It isn't merely the frivolous treatment about a holy thing that concerns me. Most worrisome is that by such lighthearted foolishness are God's people being taught. Believe it or not, this book has received rave reviews. Its back cover and front matter proclaims endorsements and recommendations by twenty-two pastors and ministry presidents and directors, many of whose names you would instantly recognize. Pastors and Christian leaders are encouraging their people to form their spiritual perspectives by listening to this kind of immature scriptural analysis.

This same author's deep and studied advice concerning the subject of universal reconciliation was quick and easy, "Universalism is a nonbiblical way for people to cope with their fear of hell. It is an escapist philosophy. Pure denial. So don't get sucked in."

Has he studied the matter, prayed and wrestled with God over it, searched the Scriptures to see what the biblical writers might have to say beyond his proof-texts?

The same author goes on to comment, "It's a kinda' double-whammy retribution reunion, lasting forever. We're talkin' bad berries...Stay out of hell. You don't want to go there. It's the pits—literally."

Neither this nor the other books I examined explored in any depth the scriptural evidence on all sides of what is a very difficult, complex, and important issue. The pat answers were given with little more than opinions and superficial anecdotes. The heartbreaking fact is, Christians are *listening* to this. It is such shallow, populist, pseudo-theology that fills the books and pulpits by which evangelicalism is forming its perspectives.

At the same time, the prayer-driven searches of people like Hannah Hurnard, and scriptural studies of depth and scholarship of men like William Barclay, and the wisdom and insight of men like Andrew Jukes, William Law, Thomas Allin, George MacDonald, and A.R. Symonds are dispensed with in a few words of "warning."

It matters very much who we listen to. It matters how they have arrived at the point of making a given declaration, and what is the Scriptural basis for the words they speak. The individuals represented in these pages are ones whose thoughts, ideas, and writings have stood the test of time.

Several of William Law's books are viewed as classics three centuries after his death. George MacDonald and Andrew Jukes are still read more than a century after their words were written. William Barclay and Hannah Hurnard's books have been in the forefront of influence within evangelicalism for the past thirty years. Their books can be found in nearly every Christian bookstore in the U.S. or Great Britain. And comment needs hardly be made about C.S. Lewis's intellect, wisdom, and contribution to Christian thought.

The mine tunnels of their writings—as I have prayerfully chipped and probed and picked away—are ones where I have discovered much to enlighten, invigorate, and challenge me, and send me ever more deeply into the Father's heart of infinite goodness and love.

I would add but one further "warning" of my own.

Neither personal search nor great scholarship, nor studying every Greek lexicon for every original meaning and nuance of every applicable word and phrase, will protect anyone from stagnant Pharisaism either. I know a number of individuals who consider themselves completely enlightened in the matter of universal reconciliation, yet sadly who are no more open-minded, forgiving, and committed to obedience to the Scriptures than those of more traditional viewpoint they so hastily condemn. I know others who are so obsessed with the study of this doctrine they can think of nothing else. It has completely taken away all sense of balance in their Christian walks. On the other hand, some of the most Christlike men and women it is a privilege to call my dear friends are lifelong believers in the orthodox view of an eternal hell. I love them and they love me, and our differences on this topic never arise. Most of them have no idea I am even interested in it, and I have no desire to raise the issue. Our love for one another completely transcends doctrinal issues. My interest in this particular one pales into insignificance alongside the value of those relationships. If I had a difficulty to resolve, it is to such individuals (on *both* sides of the fence) whose overall lives represent balance and a priority of Christlikeness to whom I would go for counsel, rather than to the acquaintances I mentioned before who are totally preoccupied with universal reconciliation above everything. Obsession nearly always leads to imbalance. And imbalance usually tends away from truth.

These are the reasons it doesn't concern me as greatly as it does some others to be *right* on such and such a point, or to *know* whether I am right or wrong. I'm far more concerned to know who God is and to try to do what he tells me.

Everything we study must be infused with and tempered by the guidance of the Holy Spirit. Otherwise we are *all* susceptible to error, Pharisaism, legalism, argumentation, judgment...no matter which side of any particular doctrinal fence we happen to be standing on. An obsession with the subject of universal reconciliation is sure to lead you off the center of Christlike living just as surely as a preoccupation with any doctrine. If we do not set ourselves to *live* the practical teachings of Jesus, then all the study in the world into these matters will only lead to lifeless intellectualism, and the worship of our own opinions, in the end.

In the quotations which follow, section headings have been added to the originals for reading ease. Likewise, I have added paragraph breaks in some of the quotations from older authors, who sometimes went on for three or four pages without them. Rather than a cumbersome system of footnotes, references are simply noted in brackets. All sources are listed in the bibliography.

I pray you enjoy the quest, and that you will be enlightened, invigorated, and challenged...and led above all to live and obey the commands and instructions of Jesus.

Part I

SCRIPTURAL EVIDENCES

PASSAGES FROM THE OLD TESTAMENT
Italics added for emphasis only

GENESIS 12:3 In you *all* the families of the earth shall be blessed. (NKJV)

1 SAMUEL 2:6   The Lord kills and he gives life, he sends down to Sheol, he can bring the dead up again. (NEB)

2 SAMUEL 14:14   For we will surely die and become like water spilled on the ground, which cannot be gathered up again. Yet God does not take away a life; but He devises means, so that His banished ones are not expelled from Him. (NKJV)

JOB 5:17-18   Happy the man whom God rebukes! Therefore do not reject the discipline of the Almighty. For, though he wounds, he will bind up; the hands that smite will heal. (NEB)

PSALM 10:15   Break the power of wickedness and wrong; hunt out all wickedness until thou canst find no more. (NEB)

PSALM 13:5   I trust in your unfailing love; my heart rejoices in your salvation. (NIV)

PSALM 16:10   You will not leave my soul in Sheol. (NKJV) ...abandon me to Sheol. (NEB)

PSALM 17:7   Show me how marvelous thy true love can be. (NEB)
PSALM 18:30   The way of God is perfect. (NEB)

PSALM 30:2-3   O Lord my God, I cried to thee and thou didst heal me. O Lord, thou has brought me up from Sheol and saved my life as I was sinking into the abyss. (NEB) ...spared me from going down into the pit. (NIV)

PSALM 30:5   For His anger is but for a moment, His favor is for life; weeping may endure for a night, but joy comes in the morning. (NKJV)

PSALM 31:7   I put my trust in the Lord. I will rejoice and be glad in thy unfailing love. (NEB)

PSALM 40:4-5   Happy is the man who makes the Lord his trust...Great things thou hast done, O Lord my God; thy wonderful purposes are *all* for our good. (NEB)

PSALM 49:15   But God will redeem my life [soul] from the grave [Sheol]; he will surely take me to himself. (NIV)

PSALM 66:10-12   For you, O God, have proved us; You have refined us as silver is refined. You brought us into the net; You laid affliction on our backs. You have caused men to ride over our heads; we went through fire and water; but You brought us out to rich fulfillment. (NKJV)

PSALM 68:18   When you ascended on high, you led captives in your train. (NIV)

PSALM 86:9   *All* the nations you have made will come and worship before you, O Lord; they will bring glory to your name. (NIV)

PSALM 86:13   For thy true love stands high above me; thou hast rescued my soul from the depths of Sheol. (NEB)

PSALM 88:10-12   Do you show your wonders to the dead? Do those who are dead rise up and praise you? Is your love declared in the grave, your faithfulness in Destruction? Are your wonders known in the place of darkness, or your righteous deeds in the land of oblivion? (NIV)

PSALM 100:5   For the Lord is good and his love endures forever; his faithfulness continues to all generations. (NIV)

PSALM 102:19-21   The Lord looked down from his sanctuary on high, from heaven he viewed the earth, to hear the groans of the prisoners and release those condemned to death. (NIV)

PSALM 103:8-14   The Lord is merciful and gracious, slow to anger, and abounding in mercy. He will not always strive with us, nor will He keep His anger forever. He has not dealt with us according to our sins, nor punished us according to our iniquities. For as the heavens are high above the earth, so great is His mercy toward those who fear Him; as far as the east is from the west, so far has he removed our transgressions from us. As a father pities his children, so the Lord pities those who fear Him. For He knows our frame; He remembers that we are dust. (NKJV)

PSALM 103:22   Praise the Lord, all his works everywhere in his dominion. (NIV)

PSALM 107:43   Let the wise man lay these things to heart, and ponder the record of the Lord's enduring love. (NEB)

PSALM 116:3-8   The cords of death bound me, Sheol [Hell] held me in its grip. Anguish and torment held me fast; so I invoked the Lord by name. "Deliver me, O Lord, I beseech thee..." Gracious is the Lord and righteous, our God is full of compassion...I was brought low and he saved me...He has rescued me from death. (NEB)

PSALM 118:1   Give thanks to the Lord, for he is good; his love endures forever. (NIV)

PSALM 119:71   How good it is for me to have been punished, to school me in thy statutes! (NEB)

PSALM 119:75   I know, O Lord, that thy decrees are just and even in punishing thou keepest faith with me. (NEB)

PSALM 138:8   The Lord will accomplish his purpose for me. Thy true love, O Lord, endures for ever; leave not thy work unfinished. (NEB)

PSALM 139:8   If I go up to the heavens, you are there; if I make my bed in Sheol, you are there. (NIV)

PSALM 145:3-17   Great is the Lord and most worthy of praise; his greatness no one can fathom...I will meditate on your wonderful works. They will tell of the power of your awesome works, and I will proclaim your great deeds. They will celebrate your abundant goodness...The Lord is gracious and compassionate, slow to anger and rich in love. The Lord is good to all; *he has compassion on all he has made.* All you have made will praise you, O Lord...They will tell of the glory of your kingdom and speak of your might, so that all men may know of your mighty acts...Your kingdom is an everlasting kingdom, and your dominion endures through all generations. The Lord is faithful to all his promises and *loving toward all he has made.* The Lord upholds all those who fall...The Lord is righteous in all his ways and loving toward all he has made. (NIV)

ECCLESIASTES 3:14   Everything God does will endure forever. (NIV)

ISAIAH 1:25   I will *thoroughly* purge away your dross and *remove all* your impurities. (NIV)

ISAIAH 14:24, 27   The Lord Almighty has sworn, "Surely, as I have planned, so it will be, and as I have purposed, so it will stand"... For the Lord Almighty has purposed, and who can thwart him? His hand is stretched out, and who can turn it back? (NIV)

ISAIAH 26:9   When your judgments come upon the earth, the people of the world learn righteousness. (NIV)

ISAIAH 46:9-10   I am God, there is no other, I am God, and there is no one like me; I reveal the end from the beginning, from ancient times I reveal what is to be: I say, "My purpose shall take effect, I will accomplish all that I please." (NEB)

ISAIAH 48:10   See, I have *refined* you...I have tested you in the furnace of affliction. (NIV)

ISAIAH 45:22-24   "Turn to me and be saved, *all* you ends of the earth. By myself I have sworn, my mouth has uttered in all integrity a word that will not be revoked: Before me *every* knee will bow; by me *every* tongue will swear. They will say of me, 'In the Lord alone are righteousness and strength.'" *All* who have raged against him will come to him and be put to shame. (NIV)

ISAIAH 54:7-8   "For a brief moment I abandoned you, but with deep compassion I will bring you back. In a surge of anger I hid my face from you for a moment, but with everlasting kindness I will have compassion on you," says the Lord your Redeemer. (NIV)

ISAIAH 55:1, 3, 5, 8-11   "Come, *all* you who are thirsty...I will make an everlasting covenant with you....Surely you will summon nations you know not, and nations that do not know you will hasten to you, because of the Lord your God, the Holy One of Israel....For my thoughts are not your thoughts, neither are your ways my ways," declares the Lord. "As the heavens are higher than the earth, so are my ways higher than your ways and my thoughts than your thoughts. As the rain and snow come down from heaven, and do not return to it without watering the earth and making it bud and flourish...so is my word that goes out from my mouth: *It will not return to me empty, but will accomplish what I desire and achieve the purpose for which I sent it.* (NIV)

JEREMIAH 23:16-22   Do not listen to what the prophets are prophesying to you...They speak visions from their own minds, not from the mouth of the Lord...But which of them has stood in the council of the Lord to see or hear his word? Who has listened to and heard his word? See, the storm of the Lord will burst out in wrath, a whirlwind swirling down on the heads of the wicked. The anger of the Lord will not turn back until he fully accomplishes the purposes of his heart. In days to come you will understand it clearly. I did not send these prophets, yet they have run with their message; I did not speak to them, yet they have prophesied. But if they had stood in my council, they would have proclaimed my words to my people. (NIV)

JEREMIAH 30:24   See what a scorching wind has gone out from the Lord, a sweeping whirlwind. It whirls round the heads of the wicked; the Lord's anger is not to be turned aside, til he has finished and achieved his heart's desire. In days to come you will understand. (NEB)

JEREMIAH 31:34   No longer will a man teach his neighbor, or a man his brother, saying, "Know the Lord," because they will all know me, from the least of them to the greatest. (NIV)

JEREMIAH 32:27, 32, 37, 40   I am the Lord, the God of all mankind. Is anything too hard for me?...The people of Israel and Judah have provoked me by all the evil they have done...I will surely gather them from all the lands where I banish them in my furious anger and great wrath...I will make an everlasting covenant with them: I will never stop doing good to them. (NIV)

LAMENTATIONS 3:31-33   For men are not cast off by the Lord forever. (NIV) Though he may punish cruelly, yet he will have compassion in the fullness of his love; he does not willingly afflict or punish any mortal man. (NEB)

EZEKIEL 18:23   Have I any desire, says the Lord God, for the death of a wicked man? Would I not rather that he should mend his ways and live? (NEB)

EZEKIEL 33:11   As I live, says the Lord God, I have no desire for the death of the wicked. (NEB)

EZEKIEL 34:11-16, 30-31   For these are the words of the Lord God: Now I myself will ask after my sheep and go in search of them. As a shepherd goes in search of his sheep when his flock is dispersed all around him, so I will go in search of my sheep and rescue them, no matter where they were scattered...I will bring them out from every nation, gather them in from other lands, and lead them home...I will search for the lost...They shall know that I, the Lord their God, am with them, and that they are my people Israel, says the Lord God. You are my flock, my people, the flock I feed, and I am your God. This is the very word of the Lord God. (NEB)

EZEKIEL 37:12   I will open your graves and bring you up from them, and restore you to the land of Israel. You shall know that I am the Lord, when I open your graves and bring you up from them, O my people. (NEB)

HOSEA 6:1   Come, let us return to the Lord; for he has torn us and will heal us, he has struck us and he will bind up our wounds. (NEB)

HOSEA 14:4, 9   I will heal their waywardness and love them freely, for my anger has turned away from them....Who is wise? He will realize these things. Who is discerning? He will understand them. The ways of the Lord are right; the righteous walk in them. (NIV)

JOEL 2:28, 3:21 And afterward, I will pour out my Spirit on *all* people...Their bloodguilt which I have not pardoned, I will pardon. (NIV)

AMOS (selections up to ch. 9):   I will send fire...I will send fire...I will send fire...I will send fire...I will send fire...Seek the Lord and live, or he will sweep through the house of Joseph like a fire...the Lord will smash the great house into pieces...I will spare my people Israel no longer...The time is ripe for my people Israel; I will spare them no longer...Are not you Israelites the same to me as the Cushites...I will destroy it from the face of the earth...In that day I will restore David's fallen tent...I will bring back my exiled people Israel. I will plant Israel in their own land, never again to be uprooted. (NIV)

MICAH 7:18-20 Who is a god like thee? Thou takest away guilt, thou passest over the sin of the remnant of thy own people, thou dost not let thy anger rage for ever but delightest in love that will not change. Once more thou wilt show us tender affection and wash out our guilt, casting all our sins into the depths of the sea. (NEB)

HABAKKUK 1:5 Look...and watch—and be utterly amazed. For I am going to do something in your days that you would not believe, even if you were told. (NIV)

HABAKKUK 2:3   The revelation awaits an appointed time; it speaks of the end and will not prove false. Though it linger, wait for it; it will certainly come and will not delay. (NIV)

HABAKKUK 2:14   For the earth will be filled with the knowledge of the glory of the Lord, as the waters cover the sea. (NIV)

ZEPHANIAH 2:11 The Lord will be awesome to them when he destroys *all* the gods of the land. The nations on *every* shore will worship him, every one in its own land. (NIV)

ZEPHANIAH 3:8-9, 15, 17, 19-20   I have decided to assemble the nations, to gather the kingdoms and to pour out my wrath on them—all my fierce anger. The whole world will be consumed by the fire of my jealous anger. *Then will I purify* the lips of the peoples, that all of them may call on the name of the Lord and serve him shoulder to shoulder....The *Lord has taken away your punishment*... he is mighty to save. He will take great delight in you, he will quiet you with his love....I will...gather those who have been scattered...At that time I will gather you; at that time I will bring you home. (NIV)

ZECHARIAH 13:9   This third I will bring into the fire; *I will refine them* like silver and test them like gold. (NIV)

MALACHI 1:11   In *every* place incense and pure offerings will be brought to my name. (NIV)

MALACHI 3:2-3   Who can endure the day of his coming? Who can stand when he appears? For he will be like a *refiner's fire* or a launderer's soap. He will sit as a *refiner* and a *purifier* of silver, he will purify the Levites and refine them like gold and silver. Then the Lord will have men who will bring offerings in righteousness. (NIV)

MALACHI 3:6-7, 10   "I the Lord do not change. So you, O descendants of Jacob, are not destroyed...Return to me, and I will return to you," says the Lord Almighty..."Test me in this," says the Lord Almighty, "and see if I will not throw open the floodgates of heaven and pour out so much blessing that you will not have room enough for it." (NIV)

MALACHI 4:1-2   "Surely the day is coming; *it will burn like a furnace.* All the arrogant and every evildoer will be stubble, and that day that is coming will set them on fire," says the Lord Almighty. "Not a root or a branch will be left to them. But for you who revere my name, the sun of righteousness will rise with healing in its wings." (NIV)

Passages From the New Testament

MATTHEW 5:43-48   You have heard that it was said, 'Love your neighbor and hate your enemy.' But I tell you: Love your enemies and pray for those who persecute you, that you may be sons of your Father in heaven. He causes his sun to rise on the evil and the good, and sends rain on the righteous and the unrighteous...Be perfect, therefore, as your heavenly Father is perfect." (NIV)

MATTHEW 16:18   "On this rock I will build my church, and the gates of hell will not overcome it." (NIV)

MATTHEW 18:11-14   "The Son of man came to save the lost. What do you think? Suppose a man has a hundred sheep. If one of these strays, does he not leave the other ninety-nine on the hillside and go in search of the one that strayed? And if he should find it, I tell you this: he is more delighted over that sheep than over the ninety-nine that never strayed. In the same way, it is not your heavenly Father's will that one of these little ones should be lost." (NEB)

MATTHEW 25:46   And these shall go away into everlasting punishment: but the righteous into life eternal. (KJV)

> Then they will go away to eternal punishment, but the righteous to eternal life. (NIV)

> And these shall go away into age-abiding correction, but the righteous into age-abiding life. (The Emphasized Bible.)

And these shall go away to punishment age-during, but the righteous to life age-during. (Young's Literal Translation)

And these last will go away into aeonian punishment, but the righteous into aeonian life. (The Twentieth Century New Testament)

And these shall be coming away into chastening eonian, yet the just into life eonian. (Concordant Literal New Testament)

και	απελευσονται	ουτοι	εις
κολασιν	αιωνιον,	οι	
δε	δικαιοι	εις	ζωην	αιωνιον.

και	απελευσονται	ουτοι	εις
kai	apeleusontai	outoi	eis
And	will go away	these	into

κολασιν	αιωνιον,	οι
Kolasin [3]	aionion, [4]	hoi
chastening ("punishment")	of/for the age ("eternal")	the

δε	δικαιοι	εις	ζωην	αιωνιον.
de	dikaioi	eis	zoen	aionion.
yet	righteous	into	life	of/for the age.

---

[3] "The word punishment in Matthew 25:46 is *kolasis* and *kolasis* originally meant the pruning of fruit trees and there is no instance in Greek where *kolasis* does not mean remedial punishment...God's punishment is always for man's cure." (William Barclay—Letter to compiler, Sept. 26, 1973)

"The word *kolasin* comes from *kolazo*, to mutilate or prune. Hence those who cling to the larger hope use this phrase to mean age-long pruning that ultimately leads to salvation of the goats, as disciplinary rather than penal. There is such a distinction as Aristotle pointed out between *moria* (vengeance) and *kolasis*...We can leave all this to the King himself who is the Judge...The word *aionios* (from *aion*, age, *aevum*, *aei*) is a difficult idea to put into language. Sometimes we have 'ages of ages' (*aiones ton aionon*). (A.T. Robertson, *Word Pictures in the New Testament*, Vol. 1, The Sunday School Board of the Southern Baptist Convention, 1930, pp. 201-02.)

[4] Literally: *aeonian, eonian*—for the age, of the age, age-lasting, age of the ages

MARK 9:48-50   ...into hell, where...the fire is not quenched. Everyone will be salted with fire. Salt is good, but if it loses its saltiness, how can you make it salty again? (NIV)

LUKE 2:10   "I bring you good news of great joy that will be for *all* people." (NIV)

LUKE 3:6   *All* mankind will see God's salvation. (NIV)

LUKE 9:54-56   When the disciples James and John saw this, they asked, "Lord, do you want us to call fire down from heaven to destroy them?" But Jesus turned and rebuked them. And he said, "You do not know what kind of spirit you are of, for the Son of Man did not come to destroy men's lives, but to save them. (NIV)

LUKE 15:2   "This man welcomes sinners..." (NIV)

LUKE 15:4   Suppose one of you has a hundred sheep and loses one of them. Does he not leave the ninety-nine in the open country and go after the lost sheep until he finds it? (NIV)

LUKE 15:20   But while he was still a long way off, his father saw him and was filled with compassion for him; he ran to his son, threw his arms around him and kissed him. (NIV)

LUKE 19:10   The Son of Man has come to seek and to save what was lost. (NIV)

JOHN 1:7   He came...that through him all men might believe. (NIV)

JOHN 1:9   This was the true light that gives light to every man who comes into the world. (NIV)

JOHN 3:17   For God did not send his Son into the world to condemn the world, but to save the world through him. (NIV)

JOHN 6:39   And this is the will of him who sent me, that I shall lose none of *all* that he has given me, but raise them up at the last day. (NIV)

JOHN 6:44-45   No one can come to me unless the Father who sent me draws him...It is written in the Prophets: "They will all be taught by God." Everyone who listens to the Father and learns from him comes to me. (NIV)

JOHN 12:32   But I, when I am lifted up from the earth, will draw *all* [5] men to myself. (NIV)

JOHN 17:2,3   For you granted him authority over all men that he might give eternal life to all those you have given him. Now this is eternal life: that they may know you, the only true God, and Jesus Christ, whom you have sent. (NIV)

JOHN 18:9   "I have not lost one of those you gave me." (NIV)

ACTS 3:19, 21   Repent, then, and turn to God, so that your sins may be wiped out, that times of refreshing may come from the Lord...He must remain in heaven until the time comes for God to restore *everything*, as he promised long ago through his holy prophets. (NIV)

> He must be received into heaven until the time of universal restoration comes, of which God spoke by his holy prophets. (NEB)

ACTS 17:30   The times of ignorance God overlooked, but now he commands all men everywhere to repent. (RSV)

ACTS 24:15   I have the same hope in God...that there will be a resurrection of both the righteous and the wicked. (NIV)

---

[5] "The word all means *all*. It is not possible for the word *all* to mean anything else, but *all*. Part of the trouble in the interpretation of Scripture is the refusal of people to take it at its face value which is nearly always right." (William Barclay—Letter to compiler, October 24, 1973)

ROMANS 5:18-19   Just as the result of one trespass was condemnation for *all* men, so also the result of one act of righteousness was justification that brings life for *all* men. For just as through the disobedience of the one man the many were made sinners, so also through the obedience of the one man the many will be made righteous. (NIV)

ROMANS 8:19-25   The creation waits in eager expectation for the sons of God to be revealed. For the creation was subjected to frustration, not by its own choice, but by the will of the one who subjected it, in hope that the creation itself will be liberated from its bondage to decay and brought into the glorious freedom of the children of God. We know that the *whole* creation has been groaning as in the pains of childbirth right up to the present time. Not only so, but we ourselves who have the firstfruits of the Spirit, groan inwardly as we wait eagerly for our adoption as sons, the redemption of our bodies. For in this hope we were saved. But hope that is seen is no hope at all. Who hopes for what he already has? But if we hope for what we do not yet have, we wait for it patiently. (NIV)

ROMANS 8:28-30   And we know that all things work together for good to those who love God, to those who are the called according to His purpose. For whom He foreknew, He also predestined to be conformed to the image of His Son, that He might be the firstborn among many brethren. Moreover whom He predestined, these He also called; whom He called, these He also justified; and whom He justified, these He also glorified. (NKJV)

ROMANS 11:16   If the firstfruit is holy, the lump is also holy; and if the root is holy, so are the branches. (NKJV)

ROMANS 11:25-26, 32   I do not want you to be ignorant of this mystery, brothers...Israel has experienced a hardening in part until the full number of Gentiles has come in. And so *all* Israel will be saved....For God has bound *all* men over to disobedience so that he may have mercy on them *all*. (NIV)

ROMANS 11:36   For from him and through him and to him are *all* things. (NIV)

ROMANS 14:9   For this very reason, Christ died and returned to life so that he might be the Lord of both the dead and the living. (NIV)

ROMANS 14:11   It is written: "'As surely as I live,' says the Lord, '*every* knee will bow before me; every tongue will confess to God.'" (NIV)

1 CORINTHIANS 12:3   Therefore I tell you that...no one can say, 'Jesus is Lord,' except by the Holy Spirit. (NIV)

1 CORINTHIANS 15:20, 22-24, 26, 28   But Christ has indeed been raised from the dead, the firstfruits of those who have fallen asleep...For as in Adam all die, so in Christ *all* will be made alive. But each in his own turn: Christ, the firstfruits; then, when he comes, those who belong to him. Then the end will come...The last enemy to be destroyed is death...so that God may be *all in all*. (NIV)

2 CORINTHIANS 5:14-15, 19   For Christ's love compels us, because we are convinced that one died for *all*, and therefore all died. And he died for *all*...God was reconciling the world to himself in Christ, not counting men's sins against them. And he has committed to us the message of reconciliation. (NIV)

EPHESIANS 1:9-10   And he made known to us the mystery of his will according to his good pleasure, which he purposed in Christ, to be put into effect when the times will have reached their fulfillment—to bring *all things* in heaven and on earth together under one head, even Christ. (NIV)

He has made known to us *his hidden purpose*—such was his will and pleasure determined beforehand in Christ—to be put into effect when the time was ripe: namely, that the universe, *all in heaven and on earth,* might be brought into a unity in Christ. (NEB)

EPHESIANS 4:8-9   "When he ascended on high, he led captives in his train and gave gifts to men." What does "he ascended" mean except that he also descended to the lower, earthly regions, the depths of the earth? (NIV)

PHILIPPIANS 2:10 ...that at the name of Jesus *every* knee should bow [6], in heaven and on earth and *under the earth,* and *every* tongue confess that Jesus Christ is Lord, to the glory of God the Father. (NIV)

COLOSSIANS 1:18-20   And he is the head of the body, the church; he is the beginning and the firstborn from among the dead, so that in everything he might have supremacy. For God was pleased...through him to reconcile to himself *all things,* whether things on earth or things in heaven, by making peace through his blood, shed on the cross. (NIV)

1 TIMOTHY 1:15   Here is a trustworthy saying that deserves full acceptance: Christ Jesus came into the world to save sinners... (NIV)

1 TIMOTHY 2:4-6   This is good and acceptable in the sight of God our Savior, *who will have all men to be saved,* and to come unto the knowledge of the truth. For there is one God, and one mediator between God and men, the man Christ Jesus, who gave himself as a ransom for *all* men, to be testified in due time. (KJV)

---

[6] "KAMPTO (καμπτω), to bend, is used especially of bending the knees in religious veneration...Phil. 2:10 [in contrast to] SUNKAMPTO (συγκαμπτω) [which] signifies to bend...down by compulsory force."(W.E. Vine, *Expository Dictionary of New Testament Words,* Fleming H. Revell, 1940.

...whose will it is that *all* men should find salvation and come to know the truth. (NEB)

1 TIMOTHY 4:10-11   We have put our hope in the living God, who is the Savior of *all* men, and especially of those who believe. (NIV)

2 TIMOTHY 1:10   ...our Savior, Christ Jesus, who has destroyed death and has brought life and immortality to light through the gospel. (NIV)

TITUS 2:11   For the grace of God has appeared for the salvation of *all* men. (RSV)

HEBREWS 2:9   But we see Jesus, who...suffered death, so that by the grace of God he might taste death for *everyone*. (NIV)

HEBREWS 9:26   He has appeared once for all at the end of the ages to do away with sin by the sacrifice of himself. (NIV)

JAMES 1:18   He chose to give us birth through the word of truth, that we might be a kind of firstfruits of *all* he created. (NIV)

1 PETER 3:18-19   For Christ died for sins once for *all*, the righteous for the unrighteous...also he went and preached to the spirits in prison who disobeyed long ago. (NIV)

1 PETER 4:6   For this is the reason the gospel was preached even to those who are now dead, so that they might...live according to God in regard to the spirit. (NIV)

2 PETER 3:9   The Lord...is longsuffering toward us, not willing that *any* should perish but that *all* should come to repentance. (NKJV)

It is not that the Lord is slow in fulfilling his promise, as some suppose, but that he is very patient with you,

because it is not his will for any to be lost, but for all to
come to repentance. (NEB)

See also Ephesians 1:9-10 and 1 Timothy 2:4—God *does*
intend to put into effect his perfect will. God's will shall
not go unaccomplished.

1 JOHN 2:2   He is the atoning sacrifice for our sins, and not only
for ours but also for the sins of *the whole world.*(NIV)

1 JOHN 3:8   The reason the Son of God appeared was to destroy
the devil's work. (NIV)

1 JOHN 4:14-15   And we have seen and testify that the Father
has sent his Son to be the Savior of the world. If anyone
acknowledges that Jesus is the Son of God, God lives in him
and he in God. (NIV)

REVELATION 1:18   Fear not...I have the keys of hell and of
death. (KJV)

REVELATION 5:13   Then I heard *every* creature in heaven and on
earth and *under the earth* and on the sea, and *all* that is in them,
singing: To him who sits on the throne and to the Lamb be
praise and honor and glory and power, for ever and ever!
(NIV)

REVELATION 15:4   Who will not fear you, O Lord, and bring
glory to your name?... *All* nations will come and worship
before you, for your righteous acts have been revealed. (NIV)

REVELATION 20:13-14   The sea gave up the dead that were in it,
and death and Hades gave up the dead that were in them, and
each person was judged according to what he had done. Then
death and Hades were thrown into the lake of fire. (NIV)

REVELATION 22:3   No longer will there be *any* curse. (NIV)

GENERAL OBSERVATIONS ABOUT
INTERPRETATION

Because the doctrine of eternal punitive hell has been a solidly entrenched pillar of Catholic and Protestant orthodoxy for so long, Bible translators skew their word choices in ways that substantiate it. This factor must be taken into account when employing most translations, where subtleties of usage, tense, and actual word meanings from the original languages disappear from sight.

Matthew 25:46, as the most obvious example, has been rendered in our English translations to support the view of eternal punishment, without a hint of the pruning, corrective, and non-eternal aspects which the Greek original conveys. We are left with a passage where "pruning for the age of the ages," or "chastening for the age," has been given as: *eternal punishment.* For a historic overview of this problem, from original manuscripts to the most modern translations, see the first two chapters of *God's Eonian Purpose,* by A.E. Loudy. [7]

Even with this difficulty, however, as is clear from the foregoing lists, numerous instances survive throughout Scripture which indicate an alternative perspective from the traditional view. Each must examine the Scriptures himself or herself and come to whatever conclusion he or she feels the Holy Spirit is leading him or her.

And where the words are too straightforward to be explained away (Philippians 2:10—that *every* knee might bow...and *every* tongue might openly confess)

---

[7] A.E. Loudy, *God's Eonian Purpose,* Concordant Publishing Concern, 1929.

commentators circuitously work their own opinions into the interpretations. In this case they would have it that such will be a "forced" bowing and an "unwilling" confession, as through clenched teeth. In explaining it thus, they ignore the Greek text at the climax of the verse ("...to the glory of God the Father" — what *glory* could such a forced confession possibly bring him?) As noted above there are two Greek words for bow: καμπτω, (KAMPTO — willing veneration and reverence,) and συγκαμπτω (SUNKAMPTO — enforced and unwilling compulsion.) The *first* (KAMPTO) is that used in Philippians 2:10.

So these skewed translations and interpretations twisted to bolster the traditional orthodoxy are a constant difficulty which the Bible student must take into account when examining the scriptural record. The reader is reminded of Dr. Barclay's statement in the note to John 12:32 — what the words actually say is nearly always right. That principle may help for the numerous preceding instances of *all* and *every* in reference to God's salvation. Unfortunately it doesn't help for mistranslations such as those familiar renderings of κολασιν (KOLASIN) and αιωνιον (AIONION).

There are proof-texts for many widely varying viewpoints. The attempt here is not to resolve every discrepancy, only to offer some of the lesser discussed scriptural passages for the reader's personal study and prayerful inquiry.

To refute either side of any argument by the proof-text method is quickly and easily done. We pray that such will not be the manner in which these lists are used. Growth and insight comes from examining the Scriptures openly and humbly, asking ourselves how various passages fit into the overall message of the Bible and into what we know of the character of both the Father and Son.

SCRIPTURAL AMBIGUITY ABOUT HELL

The concept of "hell" as an eternal place of torment for the wicked, is probably a late-first century or second-century doctrine.

Both heaven and hell remained vague in the years before Jesus' birth. The Old Testament spoke primarily of "fire," "destruction," and "restoration"— all of which intermingled ambiguously in the minds of Old Testament Jews. This confusion is evidenced by James' and John's question to the Lord in Luke 9:54. The primary word used specifically to refer to the afterlife in the Old Testament is *Sheol*, which is rendered *Hades* in Greek, which simply means *unseen* or *invisible*. The fire of destruction and the unseen place of the dead, however, were not fused into the single destination called hell until New Testament times.

None of the biblical words associated with hell, however (sheol, abyssos, hades, gehenna, katoteros— lower), conveys by internal meaning or historical etymology, a place of eternal punishment. Hades, in fact, was universally seen as a *temporary* home for the dead.

In Scripture Sheol and Hades (both which are often rendered *Hell*) merely denoted the unseen, not a place of torment and punishment. The "lake of fire" of Revelation is not the same term at all. Adlai Loudy (1893-1984) explains the etymology of the word *hell*: "It is astonishing to note the various ideas attached to the word *hell* in the English language...It is of Saxon origin, and is derived from the verb *helan*, and was spelled *hele, helle, hell, heile,* and *helan*. In this original state, the word had a very mild and harmless significance. It meant simply to *cover up, conceal,* or *hide*. The word in its primitive form is still retained, especially in the western counties of England, and means something concealed, covered, the grave. To *hele* over a thing, meant to *cover* it. Dr. Clarke says, that tiling or slating of a house is called in Cornwall, *heling,* to this day; and in Lancashire the *covers* of books are so called. Doubtless the first translators of our English Bible used the word hell in the sense of a covered or *unseen* place, the grave, or perhaps the state of death." [8]

The doctrine of hell as we know it today is a product of Jewish apocalyptic literature and post-New Testament interpreters of scant scriptural evidence—largely based on the mistranslation of Matthew 25:46, and the final chapters of Revelation.

This clarifies an extremely significant point—the fundamental orthodoxy concerning the doctrine of hell is one with roots in *tradition* and *interpretation*, not in irrefutable scriptural fact.

Jesus expanded on the Old Testament theme of "fire" and "punishment" in the afterlife (applying it to *religious* "evildoers," so to speak, more frequently than to those who would commonly be called "sinners"). His definitive statement, of course, came in Matthew 25:46. Whether he was articulating what later developed into the common view of everlasting hell, however, or something very different, remains open to conjecture.

Paul developed the doctrine of the afterlife still further, followed by John's final apocalyptic vision of the end times.

The New Testament Scriptures are confusing as well as those from the Old, in that God both adds to the truth and yet continues to hide it. The vague Old Testament view whereby fire destroyed Israel's enemies, is now revealed as the counterpart to heaven, a place where discipline, punishment, and *purification* by fire will occur. It would seem that the Spirit by which the Bible writers were inspired intended for the Old and New Testament models to be harmonized into a single unity. In such, the nature of fire (refinement and purification), and the disciplinary progression so evident throughout the entire Word of God

---

[8] Adlai Loudy, *God's Eonian Purpose*, 1929, pp. 336-38.

(*destruction* and *correction* leading to *restoration*), paves the way for a triumphant and complete picture of God's ultimate victory.

In understanding the matter, the books of Malachi and Revelation may hold equal importance. Both Testaments climax with a prophetic view of evil being, not merely punished, but *destroyed* by the fire of purification. Malachi calls it "the day of the Lord's coming."

The vision of John in Revelation, therefore, to be understood, must be seen as the New Testament fulfillment of its Old Testament counterpart. The *hell* which New Testament writers attempted to explain was none other than the *furnace of fire* prophesied by Malachi—a furnace of cleansing and purification for all people, *not* retribution toward sinners or enemies.

The following progression is offered to illuminate the potential reading of a single prophetic unfolding of God's purpose. Note that the nature of the fire is to purify, chasten, and cleanse, so that death and evil can be destroyed, out of which progression ultimately might emerge a perfect and complete worship of God by all his creation, forever.

I have decided to assemble the nations, to gather the kingdoms...The whole world will be consumed by the fire...(Zephaniah 3:8)

Then death and Hades were thrown into the lake of fire. The lake of fire is the second death. If anyone's name was not found written in the book of life, he was thrown into the lake of fire. (Revelation 20:14)

Who can endure the day of the Lord's coming? Who can stand when he appears? He will be like a refiner's fire. He will sit as a refiner and purifier of silver; he will purify the Levites and refine them like gold and silver. (Malachi 3:2-3)

Then will I purify the lips of the peoples, that all of them may call on the name of the Lord. (Zephaniah 3:9)

Then the Lord will have men who will bring offerings in righteousness, and the offerings of Judah and Jerusalem will be acceptable to the Lord, as in days gone by, as in former years... "Test me in this," says the Lord Almighty, "and see if I will not throw open the floodgates of heaven and pour out so much blessing that you will not have room enough for it." (Malachi 3:3, 10)

Then I saw a new heaven and a new earth, for the first heaven and the first earth had passed away...And I heard a loud voice from the throne saying, "Now the dwelling of God is with men, and he will live with them. They will be his people, and God himself will be with them and be their God. He will wipe every tear from their eyes. There will be no more death or mourning or crying or pain, for the old order of things has passed away. (Revelation 21:1, 3-4)

For you who revere my name, the sun of righteousness will rise with healing in its wings. (Malachi 4:2)

He said to me: "It is done. I am the Alpha and the Omega, the Beginning and the End...On each side of the river stood the tree of life...And the leaves of the tree are for the healing of the nations. No longer will there be any curse. (Revelation 21:6, 22:2-3)

At the name of Jesus every knee should bow...and every tongue confess that Jesus Christ is Lord, to the glory of God the Father. (Philippians 2:10-11)

...his name will be on their foreheads. There will be no more night. They will not need the light of a lamp or the light of the sun, for the Lord God will give them light. And they will reign for ever and ever. (Revelation 22:4-5)

ONE VERSE THEOLOGIES

It is a well-understood principle that doctrines based on a single verse of Scripture are inherently suspect. If one verse is enough, you can make the Bible say anything. ("Judas went out and hanged himself...go thou and do likewise.") One of the most obvious examples, of course, is the extensive rapture theology built around, if not a *single* verse, the combined effect of the two nearly identical passages of I Thess. 4:17 and 1 Cor. 15:52. We are all familiar with numerous examples of imbalance which result from just this pitfall.

Now while it is not true that the doctrine of eternal punitive hell is built exclusively upon Matthew 25:46, one must wonder how much support that view would have gained over the centuries had the mistranslation of that single key verse not become its central foundation stone, and had the Church instead more vigorously sought to grasp the implications of John 12:32.

Though it is not a "one verse" theology, the traditional orthodoxy of hell does not have a particularly strong or wide scriptural foundation, and rests upon but a handful of verses. This is not to say there is no scriptural evidence for this view. There clearly *is* such evidence. How reliable it is, and how verifiable are the translations in support of the various interpretations of these verses, each will have to prayerfully determine for himself or herself.

Alongside this ambiguity concerning hell, and almost entirely ignored or explained away by orthodox theologians, exists an enormous body of scriptural evidence, extending from early Old Testament times all the way to Revelation 22, which is as *unambiguous* as it is possible to be.

Compare the following two lists. Evaluate the weight of scriptural evidence on both sides of the case. And then in your own personal quest for truth...let the Word of God speak for itself.

IN SUPPORT OF PUNITIVE HELL:

Matthew 5:22   Anyone who says, "You fool!" will be in the danger of the fire of hell.

Matthew 5:29   It is better for you to lose one part of your body than for your whole body to be thrown into hell.

Matthew 7:14   Small is the gate and narrow the road that leads to life, and only a few find it.

Matthew 10:28   Rather, be afraid of the One who can destroy both soul and body in hell.

Matthew 18:8   It is better for you to enter life maimed or crippled than to have two hands or two feet and be thrown into the eternal fire.

Matthew 23:33   You snakes! You brood of vipers! How will you escape being condemned to hell?

Matthew 25:41 Depart from me...into the eternal fire prepared for the devil and his angels.

Matthew 25:46   Then they will go away into eternal punishment...

Mark 3:29   But whoever blasphemes against the Holy Spirit will never be forgiven; he is guilty of an eternal sin.

Mark 16:16 ...but whoever does not believe will be condemned.

Luke 12:5   Fear him who, after the killing of the body, has power to throw you into hell.

II Thess. 1:8-9   He will punish those who do not know God and do not obey the gospel of our Lord Jesus. They will be punished with everlasting destruction and shut out from the presence of the Lord and from the majesty of his power...

2 Peter 2:4   For if God did not spare angels when they sinned, but sent them to hell...

Jude 7   They serve as an example of those who suffer the punishment of eternal fire.

Revelation 20:10   They will be tormented day and night for ever and ever.

IN SUPPORT OF UNIVERSAL RECONCILIATION:

2 Samuel 14:14   God...devises means so that His banished ones are not expelled from him.

Psalm 16:10 ...thou wilt not abandon me to Sheol.

Psalm 116: 3-8   Sheol held me in its grip...so I invoked the Lord by name. "Deliver me, O Lord, I beseech thee..." He has rescued me and saved me from death.

Psalm 139:8 ...if I make my bed in Sheol, you are there.

Jeremiah 23:20   The anger of the Lord will not turn back until he fully accomplishes the purposes of his heart.

Lamentations 3:31   For men are not cast off by the Lord forever.

Ezekiel 18:23   Have I any desire, says the Lord, for the death of a wicked man?

Joel 2:28   I will pour out my Spirit on all people...

Matthew 16:18 ...the gates of hell will not overcome it.

Luke 3:6   All mankind will see God's salvation.

John 1:7   He came...that through him all men might believe.

John 3:17   For God did not send his Son into the world to condemn the world, but to save the world through him.

John 12:32   But I, when I am lifted up from the earth, will draw all men to myself.

Acts 3:21   He must be received into heaven until the time of universal restoration comes, of which God spoke by his holy prophets.

1 Cor. 15:22   For as in Adam all die, so in Christ all will be made alive.

Ephesians 1:9-10   He has made known to us his hidden purpose...that the universe, all in heaven and earth, might be brought into a unity in Christ.

Philippians 2:10 ...that at the name of Jesus every knee should bow...and every tongue confess that Jesus Christ is Lord.

Titus 2:11   For the grace of God has appeared for the salvation of all men.

2 Peter 3:9   ...it is not his will for any to be lost, but for all to come to repentance.

Revelation 1:18   Fear not...I have the keys of hell and death.

Revelation 22:3   No longer will there be any curse.

Part II

HISTORICAL PROPONENTS OF UNIVERSAL RECONCILIATION

THE EARLY CHURCH FATHERS

<u>Theophilus of Antioch</u> (A.D. 168) — And God showed great kindness to man, in this, that He did not suffer him to continue being in sin forever; but, as it were, by a kind of banishment, cast him out of Paradise, in order that, having by punishment expiated, within an appointed time, the sin, and having been disciplined, he should afterwards be recalled...just as a vessel, when on being fashioned it has some flaw, is remoulded or re-made, that it may become new and entire; so also it happens to man by death. For he is broken up by force, that in the resurrection he may be found whole, I mean spotless, and righteous, and immortal. [9]

<u>Iranaeus of Lyons</u> (A.D. 182) — Wherefore also He drove him out of Paradise, and removed him far from the tree of life, not because He envied him the tree of life, as some dare assert, but because He pitied him, [and desired] that he should not continue always a sinner, and that the sin which surrounded him should not be immortal, and the evil interminable and irremediable. [10]

---

[9] Andrew Jukes, *The Restitution of all Things,* Longmans, Green, & Co, London,1867, p. 177.
[10] Andrew Jukes, *The Restitution of all Things*, 1867, p. 177.

<u>Clement of Alexandria</u> (155-220)—The Lord is a propitiation, "not for our sins only," that is, of the faithful, "but also for the whole world." Therefore He indeed saves all universally; but some are converted by punishments, others by voluntary submission, thus obtaining the honour and dignity, that "to Him every knee shall bow, of things in heaven, and things in earth, and things under the earth," that is angels, and men, and souls who departed this life before His coming into the world. [11]...He punishes for their good those who are punished, whether collectively or individually. [12]

<u>Origen of Alexandria</u> (Origenes Adamantius—185-254)—He that despises the purification of the word of God, and the doctrine of the gospel, only keeps himself for dreadful and penal purifications afterwards; that so the fire of hell may purge him in torments whom neither apostolic doctrine nor gospel preaching has cleansed, according to that which is written of being "purified by fire." But how long this purification which is wrought out by penal fire shall endure, or for how many periods or ages it shall torment sinners, He only knows to whom all judgment is committed by the Father...But we must still remember that the Apostle would have this text accounted as a secret, so that the faithful and perfect may keep their perceptions of it as one of God's secrets in silence among themselves, and not divulge it everywhere to the imperfect and those less capable of receiving it. [13]

---

[11] Andrew Jukes, *The Restitution of All Things*, 1867, p. 184.

[12] Andrew Jukes, *The Restitution of All Things*, 1867, p. 184.

[13] Andrew Jukes, *The Restitution of All Things*, 1867, pp. 174-5.

(In *De Principiis*): We think, indeed, that the goodness of God, through His Christ, may recall all His creatures to one end, even His enemies being conquered and subdued...for Christ must reign until He has put all enemies under his feet. [14]

Eusebius of Caesarea (265-340) — (Writing on Psalm 2): The Son "breaking in pieces" His enemies is for the sake of remolding them, as a potter his own work, as Jeremiah 18:6 says: i.e., to restore them once again to their former state. [15]

Gregory of Nazianzus (330-389) — (In Oracles 39:19): These, if they will, may go our way, which indeed is Christ's; but if not, let them go their own way. In another place perhaps they shall be baptized with fire, that last baptism, which is not only very painful, but enduring also; which eats up, as if it were hay, all defiled matter, and consumes all vanity and vice. [16]

Gregory of Nyssa (332-398) — For it is needful that evil should some day be wholly and absolutely removed out of the circle of being. [17]

Wherefore, that at the same time liberty of free-will should be left to nature and yet the evil be purged away, the wisdom of God discovered this plan, to suffer man to do what he would, that having tasted the evil which he desired, and learning by experience for what wretchedness he had bartered away the blessings he had, he might of his own will hasten back with desire to the first blessedness...

---

[14] Dr. Jack Jacobsen, *Our Church Fathers Testify*, original date of publication unknown.

[15] Dr. Jack Jacobsen, *Our Church Fathers Testify*.

[16] Dr. Jack Jacobsen, *Our Church Fathers Testify*.

[17] Andrew Jukes, *The Restitution of All Things*, 1867, p. 179.

either being purged in this life through prayer and discipline, or after his departure hence through the furnace of cleansing fire. [18]

(In *Catechetical Orations*): Our Lord is the One who delivers man [all men], and who heals the inventor of evil himself. [19]

Ambrose Bishop of Milan (339-397) — It is necessary that all should be proved by fire, whosoever they are that desire to return to Paradise. For not in vain is it written, that, when Adam and Eve were expelled from Paradise, God placed at the outlet a flaming sword which turned every way. All therefore must pass through these fires. [20]

(Writing on Psalm 1): Our Saviour has appointed two kinds of resurrection, in accordance with which John says, in the Apocalypse, "Blessed is he that hath part in the first resurrection"; for such come to grace without the judgment. As for those who do not come to the first, but are reserved until the second resurrection, these shall be burnt, until they fulfill their appointed times, between the first and the second resurrection; or, if they should not have fulfilled them then, they shall remain still longer in punishment. [21]

There is unavoidable pain attending the removal of intruding sin. If this sin is not cured here, it is postponed to a future life. God's future judgment is the cure for the disease. [22]

---

[18] Andrew Jukes, *The Restitution of All Things*, 1867, p. 185.

[19] Dr. Jack Jacobsen, *Our Church Fathers Testify*.

[20] Andrew Jukes, *The Restitution of All Things*, 1867, p. 186.

[21] Andrew Jukes, *The Restitution of All Things*, 1867, p. 186.

[22] Hannah Hurnard, *Unveiled Glory*, p. 92.

<u>Jerome</u> (345-419)—(Writing on Zephaniah 3:8-10): The nations are gathered to the Judgment, that on them may be poured out all the wrath of the fury of the Lord, and this in pity and with a design to heal...in order that every one may return to the confession of the Lord, that in Jesus' Name every knee may bow, and every tongue may confess that He is Lord. All God's enemies shall perish, not that they cease to exist, but cease to be enemies...

(Writing on Isaiah 14:7): Our Lord descends, and was shut up in the eternal bars, in order that He might set free all who had been shut up...The Lord descended to the place of punishment and torment, in which was the rich man, in order to liberate the prisoners. [23]

<u>St. Augustine of Hippo</u> (354-430)—(*Not* a believer in universal reconciliation, wrote): There are very many in our day, who...do not believe in endless torments. [24]

<u>Theodoret of Antioch</u> (393-458)—He shows here the reason for punishment; for the Lord, the lover of men, torments us only to cure us, that He may put a stop to the course of our iniquity. [25]

---

[23] Dr. Jack Jacobsen, *Our Church Fathers Testify*.
[24] Dr. Jack Jacobsen, *Our Church Fathers Testify*.
[25] Andrew Jukes, *The Restitution of All Things*, 1867, p. 184-5.

LATER MISCELLANEOUS QUOTES

Martin Luther (1483-1546)—(In letter to Hanseu von Rechenberg, 1522): God forbid that I should limit the time of acquiring faith to the present life. In the depth of the Divine mercy there may be opportunity to win it in the futureJohann August Wilhelm Neander, the father of modern church history (1789-1850)—(*A General History of the Christian Religion and Church,* vol. 4, p. 455)—This particular doctrine was expounded and maintained with the greatest ability in works written expressly for that purpose by Gregory of Nyssa. God, he maintained, had created rational beings in order that they might be self-conscious and free vessels for the communications of the original fountain of all good. All punishments are means of purification, ordained by divine love to purge rational beings from moral evil, and to restore them back to that communion with God which corresponds to their nature. God would not have permitted the existence of evil, unless He had foreseen that by the Redemption all rational beings would in the end, according to their destination, attain to the same blessed fellowship with Himself. [26]

Johann Karl Ludwig Gieseler—1792-1854 (*Ecclesiastical History,* Vol. 1, p. 82)—The opinion of the indestructible capacity for reformation in all rational creatures, and of the finiteness of the torments of hell, was so common even in the West, and so widely diffused among opponents of Origen, that though it might not have sprung up without

---

[26] Andrew Jukes, *The Restitution of All Things,* 1867, p. 180.

the influence of his school, yet it had become quite independent of it. [27]

Ethelbert Stauffer *(New Testament Theology)* — (Writing on the early church): The primitive church never gave up the hope that in His will to save, the All-Merciful and All-Powerful God would overcome even the final "no" of the self-sufficient world.

(Writing about Paul): Paul is quite confident that there will be possibilities of salvation for men after death. It is possible...that even in the world to come, hope for the future will not cease...In 1 Corinthians 15:24, 26, Paul speaks of destruction of hostile demonic powers, which by their fall disturbed the original course of universal history. But after this great clearance, all other creatures find their way back to themselves and to their Creator in their subjection to the Son, who finally subjects Himself to the Father "that God may be all in all." [28]

Howard F. Vos *(Highlights of Church History)* — Origen believed the souls of all that God created would some day return to rest in the bosom of the Father. Those who rejected the gospel now would go to hell to experience a purifying fire which would cleanse even the wicked. [29]

Andrew Jukes — These passages show how widely the doctrine of Universal Restoration was held in the Church during the Second, Third, Fourth, Fifth Centuries...

---

[27] Andrew Jukes, *The Restitution of All Things,* 1867, p. 187.
[28] Dr. Jack Jacobsen, *Our Church Fathers Testify.*
[29] Dr. Jack Jacobsen, *Our Church Fathers Testify.*

My own conviction, the result of some acquaintance with the Fathers is, that the doctrine of Universal Restitution was held by many who in their public teaching distinctly asserted endless punishment. To take the great and good Chrysostom as an example. If we only looked at his statements as to the end of punishment, we should say that he must also hold Universal Restoration. For his doctrine is, that "if punishment were an evil to the sinner, God would not have added evils to the evil;" that "all punishment is owing to His loving us, by pains to recover us and lead us to Him, and to deliver us from sin which is worse than hell."...Yet in his sermons he repeatedly states the doctrine of everlasting punishment...His view however...and the strong feeling which he expresses as to the evil of communicating certain higher truths to the uninitiated...go far to explain why in sermons addressed to the multitude he has spoken as he has on this subject. We know however, that, spite of his popular language as to everlasting punishment, among the accusations brought against him when he was summoned to the Synod of the Oak, one distinct charge was his Origenism...

After Augustine's time, partly though his great authority, but even more in consequence of the general ignorance both of Greek and Hebrew, which for centuries prevailed in the Western Church, and which kept men from reading the Scriptures in the original languages, the doctrine of Universal Restoration was well-nigh silenced in the West until the revival of learning in the 16th century.

My own impression is that the doctrine of Purgatory, properly so called, which gradually grew up from the 5th to the 7th century, in contradistinction to the earlier view of purifying fire held by Clement of Alexandria and Origen, was a natural result of the efforts of Augustine and others to silence the doctrine of Restitution.

In the 9th century, however, John Scotus Erigena once again, and in the most decided way, bore witness to the hope of Universal Restitution. Having at an early age visited Greece, he brought back with him into the West a system of doctrine which was the fruit of a careful study of the Greek Fathers, particularly of Origen, Gregory of Nyssa, and Maximus...

Since the Reformation many of our English divines,— among the Puritans, Jeremiah White and Peter Sterry,—and in the English Church, Richard Clarke, William Law, and George Stonehouse,—in Scotland, Thomas Erskine of Linlathen and Bishop Ewing,—and among those on the Continent, Bengel, Oberlin, Hahn, and Tholuck,—have been believers in final restitution. [30]

Thomas Allin—In the present century the same steady movement continues, with ever-increasing force, in the direction of the larger hope. The name of Erskine, of Linlathen, will be familiar to many. Again, the late Bishop Wilberforce is stated on high authority to have finally "leaned to the larger hope," which his son now preaches. Other well-known names may be given as openly teaching, or sympathising with universalism, *e.g.,* Tennyson, Whittier, Bryant, Browning and Mrs. Browning, Whitman, Edna Lyall, George MacDonald, O.W. Holmes, Mrs. Oliphant, James Hinton, C. Bronte and her sister Emily, Gen. Gordon, Mrs. Mulock, Fredericka Bremer, Ellice Hopkins, Hesba Stretton, Florence Nightingale, F. Schlegel, De Quincey, Emerson, Longfellow, Mrs. Beecher Stowe...

In theology not a few names may be added, as adopting, or at least in sympathy with, the larger hope, *e.g.,* the late Bishop Ewing of Argyll, Canon Kingsley, F.D. Maurice, Dr. Cox, Baldwin Brown, Bishop Westcott, Dr. Littledale, the Bishop of Manchester, F.W. Robertson, Sir G.W. Cox, A. Jukes, Archer Gurney, Phillips Brooks,

---

[30] Andrew Jukes, *The Restitution of All Things*, 1867, p. 184, 187, 190.

Professor Mayor, Canon Farrar, Principal Caird, the Bishop of Meath, Dean Church, Neander, Martensen, Tholuck, Reuss, Schleiermacher, Bengel, Eberhard, Lavatier, J. MacLeod Campbell, the Dead of Wells, Canon Wilberforce, Pastor Oberlin, Bishop Ken, & C.

I do not represent this list as at all exhaustive, yet it is enough to prove that this movement is deep-seated, long continued, and extending itself widely amongst men of the most varied schools of thought. [31]

Billy Graham (1918-) (Interview in *Time* magazine, Nov. 15, 1993): The only thing I could say for sure is that hell means separation from God...When it comes to a literal fire, I don't preach it because I'm not sure about it. When the Scripture uses fire concerning hell, that is possibly an illustration of how terrible it's going to be—not fire but something worse.

---

[31] Thomas Allin, *Christ Triumphant, T.* T. Fisher Unwin, 1885, pp. 166-67. Allin's book , now published by Concordant Publishing Concern, contains many such quotes and references, pages 165-171.

Part III

Quotes and Essays On Universal Reconciliation

A Personal Declaration

William Barclay

A well-known Scotsman of the last century, Bible Scholar, professor, and renowned biblical expositor Dr. William Barclay (1907-1978), devoted his entire life to the study of, the attempt to understand, and the proclamation of the truths of the Scriptures. Barclay studied the classics, then divinity, and was ordained as a minister in the Church of Scotland in 1933. He pastured for thirteen years before turning his gifts to teaching. He was lecturer and professor of New Testament at the University of Glasgow for thirty years. During that time he wrote dozens of books on the Scriptures. His best-selling Daily Study Bible 17-volume commentary set on the New Testament became a classic and remains so. Barclay combined his extensive knowledge of the biblical languages and customs with a personal and straightforward style that brought the Bible to life.

Few, if any, scholars of recent times knew the Greek language and its broad, classical, literary, and biblical origins as thoroughly as this man. The following statement is mere personal conjecture, but it may well be that he knew Greek more thoroughly than any other man quoted in this discussion, on either side of the argument. D. Barclay's vast knowledge of the Bible, and the conclusions he draws about eternity, creates an intriguiguing juxtaposition of perspective when placed alongside those who vehemently claim to base their belief in everlasting torment on what they consider their superior knowledge of what the Scriptures teach. There would seem to be many who think they know the Bible better than they do.

Dr. Barclay, however, was an unpretentious man. He was not one who put on airs or sought to impress. Humility was his natural garb. He wrote simply and straightforwardly, always attempting to make the Scriptures alive and practical. He wrote to everyday Christians, not theologians.

For Barclay, universalism was not a career issue. In a long public life that saw the publication of more than fifty books, including commentaries on every book of the New Testament, nowhere else that I am aware of did he make it a point to raise this belief. He seemed aware of the divisive nature of the controversy and was unwilling to fan its flames.

Dr. Barclay is here quoted from Chapter Three ("I Believe") of his autobiography entitled, William Barclay, A Spiritual Autobiography.

I believe in God—and I believe in God the Creator...

I believe in the love of God...

I believe in prayer...I believe that real prayer is being in the presence of God...

I believe in Jesus. For me Jesus is the centre and the soul of the whole matter...

So then for me the supreme truth of Christianity is that in Jesus I see God...

I believe in Jesus, because it is only through Jesus that I know God as the Friend and Father, in whose presence I can be at home without fear, as a child with his father.

I believe in life after death...

But in one thing I would go beyond strict orthodoxy— I am a convinced universalist. I believe that in the end all men will be gathered into the love of God. In the early days Origen was the great name connected with universalism. I would believe with Origen that universalism is no easy thing. Origen believed that after death there were many who would need prolonged instruction, the sternest discipline, even the severest punishment before they were fit for the presence of God. Origen did not eliminate hell; he believed that some people would have to go to heaven via hell. He believed that even at the end of the day there would be some on whom the scars remained. He did not believe in eternal *punishment,* but he did see the possibility of eternal *penalty.* And so the choice is whether we accept God's offer and invitation willingly, or take the long and terrible way round through ages of purification.

Gregory of Nyssa offered three reasons why he believed in universalism. First, he believed in it because of the *character of God.* 'Being good, God entertains pity for fallen man; being wise, he is not ignorant of the means for his recovery.' Second, he believed in it because of *the nature of evil.* Evil must in the end be moved out of existence, 'so that the absolutely non-existent should cease to be at all'. Third, he believed in it because of *the purpose of punishment.* The purpose of punishment is always remedial. Its aim is 'to get the good separated from the evil and to attract it into the communion of blessedness'. Punishment will hurt, but it is like the fire which separates the alloy from the gold; it is like the surgery which removes the diseased thing; it is like the cautery which burns out that which cannot be removed any other way.

But I want to set down not the arguments of others but the thoughts which have persuaded me personally of universal salvation.

First, there is the fact that there are things in the New Testament which more than justify this belief. Jesus said: 'I, when I am lifted up from the earth, will draw *all* men to myself' (John 12:32). Paul writes to the Romans: 'God has consigned *all* men to disobedience that he may have mercy on all' (Rom. 11:32). He writes to the Corinthians: 'As in Adam *all* die, so also in Christ shall *all* be made alive' (1 Cor. 15: 22); and he looks to the final total triumph when God will be everything to everyone (1 Cor. 15:28). In the First Letter to Timothy we read of God 'who desires *all* men to be saved and to come to the knowledge of the truth', and of Christ Jesus 'who gave himself as a ransom for *all*'(1 Tim. 2.4-6). The New Testament itself is not in the least afraid of the word *all*.

Second, one of the key passages is Matthew 25:46 where it is said that the rejected go away to *eternal punishment,* and the righteous to eternal life. The Greek word for punishment is *kolasis,* which was not originally an ethical word at all. It originally meant the pruning of trees to make them grow better. I think it is true to say that in all Greek secular literature *kolasis* is never used of anything but remedial punishment. The word for eternal is *aionios.* The simplest way to put it is that *aionios* cannot be used properly of anyone but God; it is the word uniquely, as Plato saw it, of God. Eternal punishment is then literally that kind of remedial punishment which it befits God to give and which only God can give.

Third, I believe that it is impossible to set limits to the grace of God. I believe that not only in this world, but in any other world there may be, the grace of God is still effective, still operative, still at work. I do not believe that the operation of the grace of God is limited to this world. I believe that the grace of God is as wide as the universe.

Fourth, I believe implicitly in the ultimate and complete triumph of God, the time when all things will be subject to him, and when God will be everything to everyone (1 Cor. 15:24-28). For me this has certain consequences. If one man remains outside the love of God at the end of time, it means that that one man has defeated the love of God—and that is impossible. Further, there is only one way in which we can think of the triumph of God. If God was no more than a King or Judge, then it would be possible to speak of his triumph, if his enemies were agonising in hell or were totally and completely obliterated and wiped out. But God is not only King and Judge, God is *Father*—he is indeed Father more than anything else. No father could be happy while there were members of his family for ever in agony. No father would count it a triumph to obliterate the disobedient members of his family. The only triumph a father can know is to have all his family back home. The only victory love can enjoy is the day when its offer of love is answered by the return of love. The only possible final triumph is a universe loved by and in love with God.

Two objections are commonly levelled against universalism. It is claimed that it takes the iron out of Christianity because it removes the threat. No longer can the sinner be dangled over the pit of hell. No longer can what Burns called 'the hangman's whip' of fear of hell be threateningly cracked over the sinner. But the kind of universalism in which I believe has not simply obliterated hell and said that everything will be all right for everyone; it has stated grimly that, if you will have it so, you can go to heaven via hell. The threat is still there. Further, it is claimed that universalism does away with free-will. Early on in his thought Origen has the astonishing picture of a universe in which the free-will always obtains and in which to the end of time a man can fall from heaven and rise from hell; but in the end he came to think in terms of a final decision. What is forgotten is that God has eternity to work in. It is a question of God using an eternity of persuasion and appeal until the hardest heart breaks down and the most stubborn sinner repents.

As I see it, nothing less than a world is enough for the love of God. [32]

---

[32] William Barclay, *A Spiritual Autobiography*, William B. Eerdmans, 1975, Ch. 3.

ON FREE WILL

A.R. Symonds

The Rev. A.R. Symonds was a nineteenth century Oxford author about whom I am sorry to say I have not been able to locate much information. I happened to encounter a hundred year old copy of his book, The Ultimate Reconciliation and Subjection Of All Souls To God Under the Kingdom Of Christ (1878), and quote from it here.

THE OBJECTION OF FREE WILL

At this point in the argument an obvious objection presents itself, and must be considered. That objection may be fairly stated in the following form:

"Man is a free agent, and as such there must be acceptance on
his part of the terms of salvation. Salvation is a product of the co-operation of the human will with the divine will. If, then, in the exercise of his free will a man has resisted the divine will throughout his present life, is it not quite conceivable that he may continue that resistance throughout eternity. In such a case, perdition would be simply a man's own act, and *ipso facto* must be eternal. God forces damnation on no man, neither does He force salvation on any man. Christ did indeed die for all,

salvation therefore, is possible for all, all who *will* may be saved; hence, if any are not saved it is because they will not. God is willing, indeed, that all should be saved, but He doth not coerce the will of any."

Under one form or other this objection is the one most frequently, perhaps, advanced by thoughtful men, as that which hinders their accepting, what otherwise they would have been disposed to accept, the doctrine of the ultimate subjection of all souls to God, deeming it to involve a coercing of the free will of man. But in the use of this word "coerce" there lurks, I think, a misconception; if this be removed, the objection itself will lose much of its point and plausibility. If by "coerce" be meant the bringing to bear a kind of mechanical force, absolutely overpowering the human will, and so compelling it as, in effect, to cause the actings of a man to be no longer the result of the exercise of his own will, for such an exertion of the divine will over the human will, neither is there warrant to hope, nor indeed would it be right to hope, seeing that a submission so produced would have no moral worth.

CONSTRAINING WITHOUT COERCION

But that the divine will may be so brought to bear on the human will as to *constrain* though not to *compel* it, so attracting, drawing and persuading it, as to *win* it to subjection, so influencing it as, while not destroying or impairing its freedom, to bring at last every man *of his own will* to submit himself to God's will, for this, I contend, there is real ground of hope, not only in the direct Scripture testimony which has been already adduced, and in the *a priori* presumptions which the facts of the case afford, but in what we ourselves know and have felt of the working of divine grace, as it is *now* exhibited in the conversion of souls to God.

For what, let it be asked, is the history of any true conversion of a soul to God? It is the history of a human will so wrought upon by divine grace as to overcome its perversity, and to turn it from its bias to evil in the direction of good. The uniform experience and the unvarying confession of every truly converted man is expressed in the memorable words of St. Paul, "By the grace of God I am what I am." The operations of divine grace in effecting conversion are, indeed, infinitely diverse, both in manner and degree, corresponding to the infinite variety in the condition of the human will and of the circumstances affecting it. Nevertheless, of every soul truly converted to God, whether in childhood, in manhood, or in old age, whether under circumstances favourable or adverse, whether after an aggravated course of sin or in comparative innocence of evil, whether in an obstinate and hardened state of mind or in one more open and predisposed to conviction, of each and all alike will the acknowledgment be one and the same, "Of my own will, and left to myself, I should never have turned to God; I am what I am by the grace of God."...

At this point we are confronted with a startling and a stupendous fact. Out of the whole mass of human beings which have been born into the world since its creation, two thirds at least I suppose, at any rate millions upon millions, have passed away from this life without any communication to them, either under the law or under the gospel, of the way of salvation...Place this fact alongside of the inspired declaration that God willeth all men to be saved and to come to the knowledge of the truth, and is not the inference absolutely irresistible, that as on the one hand the divine will cannot be thwarted, but must in one way or other take effect; and as on the other hand myriads of human souls have never in the *present* life come within range of either the law of the Old Testament, or the gospel of the New, therefore assuredly will that grace, which bringeth salvation to all men, be brought to bear upon them in ages yet to come?

THE VARIABLE OPERATION OF GRACE

Another fact confronts us. Even those within the pale of the visible Church, and within the range and means of grace, how varied both in time of visitation, and in degree of force and efficacy, is the operation of grace...Some are constantly and continuously subject to constraining movements within, and to hallowing influences from without, while others pass through life and out of it scarcely conscious of any special strivings and searchings of heart. Two men, alike unconverted, listen to the same sermon; to one the word comes in power and demonstration of the Spirit so that being pricked in his heart, he cries out, "What must I do to be saved?"; the other departs untouched, unmoved...

Instances like these might be multiplied to any extent, all illustrating the same truth, that converting grace is sovereign grace, "that it is not of him that willeth nor of him that runneth, but of God that hath mercy"...In each instance, only to grace working after the counsel of the divine will can conversion be attributed. Yet in no case is there such coercion of the will as to violate its freedom, but in each and all it is grace operating on the human will with convincing and persuasive efficacy, disposing, constraining, and enabling it to turn to God.

At what point and in what way the human will meets and co-operates with the divine will, we cannot and we care not to explain. This only we know...that conversion is the work of grace...Why grace operates effectually in some cases and not in others, we can give no other reason than that so it pleaseth Him "who worketh all things after the counsel of his own will." (Ephesians 1:11)

The whole process of converting grace, both in its providential and spiritual operation, is a manifestation of the *election* of grace. Shrink as some may from this doctrine, they must at least recognize providential selection in the simple fact that to some the gospel is offered, while others never hear of it. What is this but election of grace? That election, however, is not, as Calvinism teaches, the election of a few to eternal life *to the exclusion of the rest*, but...the election of some, in the present era of Christ's kingdom, to the dignity and duty of the first-born, to become in another era, as princes and priests to God, coadjutors of the Saviour King in the recovery of a fallen world, and in the subjection of all souls to his rule.

The objection to the doctrine of election, as stated by Calvinists, lies in the assumption that the operation of saving grace is restricted to the present life of man, and that consequently all souls not saved before death are eternally damned; an assumption as dishonouring to divine justice and mercy as it is revolting and repulsive to the reason and moral sense of man. The purpose of redemption is the purpose of the ages, a purpose to be wrought out and consummated in successive epochs...

Are we, then, to believe, it may be said, that God will save in spite of a man's will not to be saved?

And who, I ask, have been saved, except more or less in contrariety to their own will; at all events have not many been saved, most willful resisters of grace, saved glaringly against their own will? If these, then why not others?

Let me put a case. Suppose we were to see a man trying to drown himself, should we not endeavour to rescue him, yea, though he should persist in his attempt, and, in his determination to drown himself, repel ever so much our efforts to save him? If able to do it, should we not feel *bound* to save him, even against his own will? Were we not to do so, did we say "let the man drown himself if he will," should we not deservedly be pronounced cruel and inhuman.

Are we more kind and right-judging than God?

Shall we account it an imperative obligation in such a case to effect a rescue, and shall we deem it a thing inconceivable that the All Merciful should save sinners from their sin, whatever their resistance to his will?

If so, then how is that precept to be understood, "Be ye merciful, be ye perfect, even as your Father which is in heaven is merciful and perfect." (Matthew 5:48; Luke 6:36) [33]

---

[33] A.R. Symonds, *The Ultimate Reconciliation and Subjection Of All Souls To God Under the Kingdom Of Christ*, 1878, pp. 37-38, 47-52.

ONE WOMAN'S SEARCH

Hannah Hurnard

Hannah Hurnard (1905-1990) is well-known for her best-selling Hind's Feet On High Places and Mountains Of Spices. Yet very little is known by her vast readership about her personal life. Born, raised, and educated in England, Miss Hurnard became an independent missionary in Israel as a young woman, where she remained for more than fifty years. During that time she authored more than twenty books. The following excerpts are taken from her small volume Unveiled Glory, 1956, and recount her personal struggle and search to find truth in the Scriptures.

The things which I see now are so astonishingly and blessedly unlike some of my earlier conceptions of certain truths, and the revolution has been so great in heart and soul and mind, and is the outcome of such a long and hidden process, that it really seems necessary to give some explanation of how such a revolution came about.

The first clear link in this chain of events goes back to a certain night during the years of terrorism in Palestine...Those were perilous times...here was this poor Moslem woman desperately needing medical help, and we decided to break curfew, steal away under cover of darkness and try to get through to the Mission Hospital away on the hills of Nazareth, trusting that we would meet none of the marauding gangs...

It was a strange, tense drive...As the moon at last rose over the great shoulder of Mount Tabor, the woman became unconscious...we went rushing as speedily as possible up the hairpin bends of the hills, until, at last, we reached the Mission Hospital. Then, just as the stretcher bearers gently carried the unconscious woman into the operating theatre, she died.

That night, alone in my room at the hospital, as I thought of the desperate drive which had been all in vain, I found myself confronted for the first time in my life by a question which I had never fully faced up to before.

What happens after death to those who never in their lifetime have had the opportunity to hear the Gospel and who die knowing nothing at all about the Saviour?

Here was this young Moslem woman, not more that twenty years old, whom we had tried desperately to save from death. She had never heard the Gospel and we hoped she might have had the chance to hear it in the Mission Hospital. Now she had died. What *was* happening to her?

The teaching upon this matter in which I had been brought up was most emphatic. *All such were lost*—lost eternally. For there could be no chance anywhere nor at any time except during this life on earth, for anyone to hear the Gospel. That was why it was so supremely important that there should be missionaries who would go to the ends of the earth to make known "to every creature" the Good News, the glorious news of the loving Saviour Who died for everyone; the message of the One true God "Who so loved the world that He gave His only begotten Son, that whosoever believeth on Him should not perish, but have everlasting life" —

Unless, alas, they were born and lived where they never had the chance to hear about Him and so could not believe on Him —

A God and Saviour, in fact, who was all love and forgiveness and willing to receive the worst and most ignorant sinner until the very last flicker of their breath and earthly consciousness, but Who, one moment after they died, would turn away—for ever turn away—saying sadly, "Too late. There is no further chance now. I can no longer undertake to save this lost soul for whom I died."

When I got to that point in my thoughts, alone there in the hospital room, and thought of how I myself had been so infinitely privileged and blessed to be born into a Christian home in a Christian land, I looked up into the face of the Lord Who so loved me and that Moslem woman also, I remembered that He had died for us both, and I said to Him:

"Lord, help me to understand. Have You really ceased to love this ignorant Moslem woman, my sister human being, and yet so terribly less privileged than myself? Can You really do nothing for her now? We had no chance to tell her even one word about You. Does this mean that she must really go out into the darkness and be lost for ever and ever? Then, Lord, why did You let her be born, and all the countless other billions of ignorant men and women and children around the world in all ages, who never heard the Gospel? They began by being 'lost' and they end up by being 'lost eternally'..."

Then it seemed to me that very gently and quietly the Lord about Whom I had supposed that I must believe such things, said:

"Hannah, when you were driving that poor, ignorant woman to the hospital, you were absolutely certain that I Myself was with you, and that My love and pity and compassion were encompassing you all. Then can you really believe that one moment after she died, I, Who had constrained you to risk the snipers and the raiders, then withdrew from her My compassion and My love, and My power to save her? Must you not think that I, Who was with you, although unseen, would be the very first One whom that poor ignorant soul would see when she left the body? And that she, who had never heard of Me while she was living on earth, would find Me close beside her, offering her the love and forgiveness and the 'Good News' of the Gospel which she had never had the chance to hear?"

"Lord," I whispered, "it does not say so in the Bible, but just the opposite. It says that she and those like her, are lost—are lost for ever."

"It does not say so in the Bible!" said the Good Shepherd of the sheep. "Why, Hannah, have you never read of the Shepherd Who goeth after the sheep *until He find it?*" (Luke 15:4)...Trust that woman on whom you had compassion enough to risk that drive, trust her to ME...I have such love for her that I went to the cross for her."

Next morning...I watched the young husband and the mourners carry away the pitiful, blanket-wrapped figure, to lay it, just as it was, in the grave, I found all my questioning sorrow turned into joy and thankfulness. For what we had been unable to tell her while she lay unconscious in the car, and what she had never lived to hear at the hospital, I was sure that she now heard in some way from the lips of the One Who was Himself her Creator, her Lover and her Redeemer. I thought with a new and lovely understanding of the poor beggar Lazarus...

From that night I laid aside...with adoring thankfulness, the conception of a God Who so loved fallen sinners that He died for them, but Who, if they never heard about Him, allowed them to "perish" and to be tormented in hell and to be separated from Him for ever.

But I kept silent about the matter because, when on occasions I tried to tell some of my friends about this experience, they thought that it completely contradicted the Scriptures, and that even to suggest such a thing would be dangerous, as it would most likely cut the nerve of missionary effort...Why, they asked, should Christ have said, "He that believeth, and is baptised, shall be saved; but he that believeth not, shall be damned." (Mark 16:16.)

I didn't know the answer to those questions...

That was as far as I could see in those days: just the simple certainty that no soul created by the "faithful Creator" would be lost eternally nor be sent to an endless hell, because never having heard the Gospel, they had never "believed on the Lord Jesus Christ."...I was brought up in a circle of Christians in which these things were honestly and sincerely believed. And there are many Christians today who still sincerely believe them and fear to give them up because they are sure that the Scriptures *do* teach them that and it would be disloyal to the Word of God to suggest anything else.

The second link in this "chain of events", by which gradually the veil was drawn aside in my understanding...I found myself obliged to begin asking many, many questions which, until then, had never occurred to me, but which now took on the most tremendous importance...

As I thought and prayed about it I found myself obliged to ask in all honesty, Are all human beings really free to exercise their free will?...

As I thought...it broke upon my understanding in an almost overwhelming way that, though all human beings potentially possess free will, the actual fact is that multitudes of them are born into conditions where they will not be free to exercise that "free will" because they will be the slaves of sin even in childhood. Whereas I, like others, was born into an environment in which it is infinitely easier to choose good and to respond to the Saviour....

Then I began to look up and study various passages in the Scriptures which until then I had read quite carelessly and unthinkingly...

It is difficult for me to describe the almost overwhelming impression of astonishment and thankfulness which... [my] discover[ies] made upon me.

You see, all my Christian life I had been taught to suspect the term "The universal Fatherhood of God." No, He was the Father only of such as "stirred themselves up to call upon Him" in penitence and faith. Not until we are born of the Spirit have we the right, I had always supposed, to call him Father. Yet here was Isaiah the prophet stating exactly the contrary...

As these things began to take clearer shape in my mind...I found my heart crying out in anguish:

Why?—why, O God our Maker? why did You ever create human beings in *Your own image*...How can You allow them to be born, countless millions of them...only and for the torments of *an endless hell?* And, worst of all, *to be fixed in a state of hopeless evil for ever?*

How could the Bible possibly speak of the perfect victory of God our Creator Who loves righteousness and cannot bear evil, if that victory really means that He cannot bring His own creatures at last to hate evil as He hates it, but must confirm multitudes, indeed the majority of them, in their choice of evil for ever and ever?

Surely the only thing which perfect Love and perfect Righteousness can consider worthy of the name of victory is to be able to win *all* to hate and forsake evil, for ever beyond the reach of any temptation to return to it again? What sort of a victory is it to be able only to subdue evil and prevent it harming any but those who choose it, and to be *unable* to bring human souls to abominate it and desire to forsake it, so that the evil itself ceases to exist?...

The clearer these things presented themselves to my mind, the more plainly I saw that any supposed interpretation of the teaching of the Holy Scriptures which taught otherwise must be mistaken interpretations, because they are totally at variance to the revelation of a Holy God Who loves righteousness and hates evil, and Who only permits its existence temporarily that all creatures may learn to hate it and turn from it for ever.

Then my thoughts turned to all those verses in the Bible...

The more I prayed over Romans 9, the more surprised I became!...Isaiah 45:9-12...

What does all this mean?...I had always supposed that this verse meant there would be a *forced* submission to God in the end...

But what sort of victory could that be to the Father heart of God...

...then has God really no loving and redemptive purposes for such immortal souls after they leave their bodies?...If it is almost impossible to get some really zealous and convinced "Conservative Christians" to open their minds even a tiny crack to admit some new aspect of Truth which may have been mislaid in their particular section of the Church, how much harder must it be for non-Christian people to open their minds to receive the Gospel...

As all these questions came surging into my mind...I was continually oppressed with the fear that all this was dreadful heresy and that these were questions which cast suspicion on the verity of the inspired Scriptures. But still, honesty, yes, and love to the Lord and intense longing to know Him better and to be freed from any false distortions of His character, impelled me to go on praying and seeking for light, and asking questions! For does not the Creator Who gave us minds, *want* us to ask questions when once we really begin to see what we are committing ourselves to, when we believe things about God which must be a distortion both of His justice and His love?...

I found that *this* was the heart of the problem. All the questions really boiled down to one question:

Do the inspired Scriptures really teach what I had for so long supposed I must believe? Or had I been believing "traditions of men" which were not a true interpretation of the Scriptures themselves?...oh, the joy, and relief and inexpressible thankfulness it would be to be free to believe about God the things which alone seemed worthy of Him and in harmony with the lovely revelation of Him given by Jesus Christ...

"Too good to be true!" That was what it really boiled down to...

Oh, how many were the doubts and objections and fears of accepting errors which arise in my mind. And then, one night...I came across a book by William Law...and there I began to find the lovely, liberating answer to the whole question, although all the details, of course, were not made plain immediately...

I am now fully persuaded that as God is Love there can be in Him no wrath such as we conceive of wrath, or any possibility that He will condemn His own creatures to unending destruction, but I must still ask, *What am I to do with all the passages of Scripture which seem to assert the very contrary?*

The Scriptures of course *do* teach that there is a hell...yet there are many other passages which most emphatically state that, in the end, God will completely triumph over evil...

What astonishing questioning this discovery led to...

Once it became clear to my mind that none of the passages concerning this matter were to be explained away, but all must be accepted and a higher truth discovered which would reconcile them all, impossible as this seemed, then I made another discovery...

I discovered that there is not one single verse in the Scriptures which uses the words "everlasting," "eternal," or "for ever and ever" in connection with hell. That is to say, in no single verse translated in English by the word hell referring to Gehenna, Sheol, or Hades the Pit, or the grave, is any word used which even hints that these places, or conditions, are endless, but there are several which definitely speak of being delivered out of hell. Therefore

Hell and Hades (the place of departed spirits) cannot even be assumed to be endless; they must be TEMPORARY...

...if it is clearly stated that in the end "death and hell" are actually cast into the lake of fire for complete destruction, then it is obvious that they must play some vital and important role in preparing for God's Final Victory and for the "restitution of all things."...

...hell must surely be the terrible experience of being allowed to reap the full harvest of sin and its awful fruits of misery, ruin and torment. Holy Love would so thankfully spare every single soul such an experience, but if there is no other way by which men can be brought to hate and abominate sin and to turn from it willingly and for ever, then they will be permitted to reap that awful harvest. Surely all whom Holy Love permits to pass through that appalling experience will learn at last to turn from evil with utmost horror and loathing, safe for ever after from any future temptation to plunge into it again!

It was then, at last, that a veil seemed drawn away completely from my understanding and I beheld the glory which has been unveiled to us by the Lord Jesus Christ in His resurrection from the dead, by which he demonstrated His complete and perfect victory over sin, death and hell and all the works of the Devil. I also began to see what this glorious victory means for the *whole body of mankind*...

I have looked upon the Face of Love Himself, and as a result all my earlier conceptions of the nature and character of God and His purposes for Mankind have been swallowed up. It feels almost as though I have seen a new God altogether, but I know, of course, that the real fact is I have seen the true God in a new way—in the Face of the *Risen* Lord and Saviour Jesus Christ. As a result "old things have passed away and all things have become new." [34]

---

[34] Hannah Hurnard, *Unveiled Glory*, 1956, pp. 5-30.

ON SCRIPTURAL FIRE

George MacDonald

Among the many authors whose words support a belief in God's complete victory, none perhaps is more persistent in refusing to make an overt declaration of such a position than nineteenth century Scottish preacher, poet, and novelist George MacDonald (1824-1905), whose works during the last forty years have enjoyed a remarkable renaissance, most particularly in the United States and Germany. A virtual unknown forty years ago in spite of C.S. Lewis's repeated references to MacDonald as his "master," more than a hundred editions of MacDonald's books have been re-issued during the past several decades, stimulating great interest in the views of this often controversial writer.

Raised in the strict Calvinism of nineteenth century Scotland, MacDonald's own "personal search" is recounted in his biography, George MacDonald, Scotland's Beloved Storyteller.

My own feeling is that MacDonald's reluctance to make a definitive statement stems from his view that to make universal reconciliation an issue upon which much energy is spent would be divisive and thus detrimental to both unbelievers and immature believers.

His reluctance, as I read it, additionally stemmed from the fact that universal reconciliation was for him merely one small aspect of an entire outlook that had God himself at its core rather than any specific "doctrine." Whatever specific form his personal beliefs on the matter took, like his fellow Scotsman William Barclay, neither for MacDonald was this a "career issue." He did not engage in written debate on the matter, or contribute anything that would tend toward disunity in the body of Christ. MacDonald writes: "Say if you will that I fear to show my opinion...I will not then tell you what I think, but I will tell any man who cares to hear it what I believe...I desire to wake no dispute, will myself dispute with no man..."

MacDonald offers unique insight particularly when addressing the nature of the purifying fires and the justice of God, and quotes from him are therefore offered in some length on these two topics in particular.

INEXORABLE CONSUMING LOVE

Nothing is inexorable but love...Love is one, and love is changeless.

For love loves into purity. Love has ever in view the absolute loveliness of that which it beholds...There is nothing eternal but that which loves and can be loved, and love is ever climbing towards the consummation when such shall be the universe, imperishable, divine.

Therefore all that is not beautiful in the beloved, all that comes between and is not of love's kind, must be destroyed.

And our God is a consuming fire.

If this be hard to understand, it is as the simple, absolute truth is hard to understand...

For this vision of truth God has been working for ages of ages...and for this will the patience of God labour while there is yet a human soul whose eyes have not been opened, whose child-heart has not yet been born in him...let us have grace to serve the Consuming our God, with divine fear...It is the nature of God, so terribly pure that it destroys all that is not pure as fire, which demands like purity in our worship. He will have purity. It is not that the fire will burn us if we do not worship thus; but that the fire will burn us until we worship thus; yea, will go on burning within us after all that is foreign to it has yielded to its force, no longer with pain and consuming, but as the highest consciousness of life, the presence of God. When evil, which alone is consumable, shall have passed away in his fire from the dwellers in the immovable kingdom, the nature of man shall look the nature of God in the face, and his fear shall then be pure....

Yea, the fear of God will cause a man to flee, not from him, but from himself; not from him, but to him, the Father of himself, in terror lest he should do him wrong or his neighbour wrong....

The symbol of the consuming fire would seem to have been suggested to the writer by the fire that burned on the mountain of the old law. That fire was part of the revelation of God there made to the Israelites...But the same symbol employed by a writer of the New Testament should mean more, not than it meant before, but than it was before employed to express; for it could not have been employed to express more than it was possible for them to perceive...How should they think of purification by fire? They had yet no such condition of mind as could generate such a thought. And if they had had the thought, the notion of the suffering involved would soon have overwhelmed the notion of purification....Fear was that for which they were fit. They had no worship for any being of whom they had not to be afraid.

Was then this show upon Mount Sinai...not a true revelation of God?...

No revelation can be other than partial...For what revelation, other than a partial, can the highest spiritual condition receive of the infinite God? But it is not therefore untrue because it is partial. Relatively to a lower condition of the receiver, a more partial revelation might be truer than that would be which constituted a fuller revelation to one in a higher condition; for the former might reveal much to him, the latter might reveal nothing. Only, whatever it might reveal, if its nature were such as to preclude development and growth, thus chaining the man to its incompleteness, it would be but a false revelation fighting against all the divine laws of human existence. The true revelation rouses the desire to know more by the truth of its incompleteness....

The worship of fear is true, although very low; and though not acceptable to God in itself, yet even in his sight it is precious. For he regards men not as they are merely, but as they shall be; not as they shall be merely, but as they are now growing, or capable of growing, towards that image after which he made them that they might grow to it. Therefore a thousand stages, each in itself all but valueless, are of inestimable worth as the necessary and connected gradations of an infinite progress. A condition which of declension would indicate a devil, may of growth indicate a saint....

THE FIRE BURNS CLEAN

But we shall find that this very revelation of fire is itself, in a higher sense, true to the mind of the rejoicing saint as to the mind of the trembling sinner. For the former sees farther into the meaning of the fire, and knows better what it will do to him. It is a symbol which needed not to be superseded, only unfolded.

While men take part *with* their sins...how can they understand that the lightning word is a Saviour, that word which pierces to the dividing between the man and the evil, which will slay the sin and give life to the sinner? Can it be any comfort to them to be told that God loves them so that he will burn them clean. Can the cleansing of the fire appear to them anything beyond what it must always, more or less, be—a process of torture?

They do not want to be clean, and they cannot bear to be tortured. Can they then do other, or can we desire that they should do other, than fear God, even with the fear of the wicked, until they learn to love him with the love of the holy. To them Mount Sinai is crowned with the signs of vengeance.

And is not God ready to do unto them even as they fear, though with another feeling and a different end from any which they are capable of supposing?

He is against sin: in so far as, and while, they and sin are one, he is against them—against their desires, their aims, their fears, and their hopes; and thus he is altogether and always for them.

That thunder and lightning and tempest, that blackness torn with the sound of a trumpet, that visible horror billowed with the voice of words, was all but a faint image to the senses of the slaves of what God thinks and feels against vileness and selfishness...that so the stupid people, fearing somewhat to do as they would, might leave a little room for that grace to grow in them, which would at length make them see that evil, and not fire, is the fearful thing; yea, so transform them that they would gladly rush up into the trumpet-blast of Sinai to escape the flutes around the golden calf.

Could they have understood this, they would have needed no Mount Sinai. It was a true, and of necessity a partial revelation—partial in order to be true....

May it not then hurt to say that God is Love, all love, and nothing other than love? It is not enough to answer that such is the truth, even granted that it is...For when we say that God is Love, do we teach men that their fear of him is groundless? No. As much as they fear will come upon them, possibly far more. But there is something beyond their fear—a divine fate which they cannot withstand...The wrath will consume what they *call* themselves; so that the selves God made shall appear, coming out with tenfold consciousness of being....They will know that now first are they fully themselves...That which they thought themselves shall have vanished...For that which cannot be shaken shall remain. That which is immortal in God shall remain in man. The death that is in them shall be consumed.

THE DESTRUCTIBLE SHALL BE DESTROYED

It is the law of Nature—that is, the law of God—that all that is destructible shall be destroyed....The destructible must be burned out of it, or begin to be burned out of it, before it can *partake* of eternal life. When that is all burnt away and gone, then it has eternal life. Or rather, when the fire of eternal life has possessed a man, then the destructible is gone utterly, and he is pure.

Many a man's work must be burned, and by that very burning he may be saved—"so as by fire."

Away in smoke go the lordships, the Rabbihoods of the world, and the man who acquiesces in the burning is saved by the fire; for it has destroyed the destructible, which is the vantage point of the deathly, which would destroy both body and soul in hell. If still he cling to that which can be burned, the burning goes on deeper and deeper into his bosom, till it reaches the roots of the falsehood that enslaves him—possibly by looking like the truth.

The man who loves God, and is not yet pure, courts the burning of God. Nor is it always torture. The fire shows itself sometimes only as light—still it will be fire of purifying. The consuming fire is just the original, the active form of Purity,—that which makes pure, that which is indeed Love, the creative energy of God. Without purity there can be as no creation so no persistence. That which is not pure is corruptible, and corruption cannot inherit incorruption.

The man whose deeds are evil, fears the burning. But the burning will not come the less that he fears it or denies it. Escape is hopeless. For Love is inexorable. Our God is a consuming fire. He shall not come out till he has paid the uttermost farthing.

THE OUTER DARKNESS WHERE EVERY FARTHING MUST BE PAID

If the man resists the burning of God, the consuming fire of Love, a terrible doom awaits him, and its day will come. He shall be cast into the outer darkness who hates the fire of God. What sick dismay shall then seize upon him! For let a man think and care ever so little about God, he does not therefore exist without God....God gives him himself, though he knows it not. But when God withdraws from a man...then will he listen in agony for the faintest sound of life from the closed door; then...he will be ready to rush into the very heart of the Consuming Fire to know life....Imagination cannot mislead us into too much horror of being without God—that one living death....The outer darkness is but the most dreadful form of the consuming fire—the fire without light—the darkness visible, the black flame. God hath withdrawn himself, but not lost his hold. His face is turned away, but his hand is laid upon him still. His heart has ceased to beat into the man's heart, but he keeps him alive by his fire. [35]

THE LAST FARTHING

We have a good while given us to pay, but a crisis will come...comes always sooner than those expect it who are not ready for it—a crisis when the demand unyielded will be followed by prison.

The same holds with every demand of God: by refusing to pay, the man makes an adversary who will compel him—and that for the man's own sake. If you or your life say, "I will not," then he will see to it. There is a prison, and the one thing we know about that prison is, that its doors

---

[35] George MacDonald, *Unspoken Sermons First Series*, 1867, "The Consuming Fire," pp. 27-48 of the Sunrise Books edition, 1988.

do not open until entire satisfaction is rendered, the last farthing paid.

The main debts whose payment God demands are those which lie at the root of all right, those we owe in mind, and soul, and being. Whatever in us can be or make an adversary, whatever could prevent us from doing the will of God, or from agreeing with our fellow—all must be yielded. Our every relation, both to God and our fellow, must be acknowledged heartily, met as a reality...

If the man accepts the will of God, he is the child of the Father, the whole power and wealth of the Father is for him, and the uttermost farthing will easily be paid. If the man denies the debt, or acknowledging does nothing towards paying it, then—at last—the prison!

God in the dark can make a man thirst for the light, who never in the light sought but the dark. The cells of the prison may differ in the degree of darkness; but they are all alike in this, that not a door opens but to payment...

I think I have seen from afar something of the final prison of all, the innermost cell of the debtor of the universe; I will endeavor to convey what I think it may be.

It is the vast outside; the ghastly dark beyond the gates of the city of which God is the light—where the evil dogs go ranging, silent as the dark, for there is no sound any more than sight. The time of signs is over. Every sense has its signs, and they were all misused: there is no sense, no sign more—nothing now by means of which to believe.

The man wakes from the final struggle of death, in absolute loneliness—such a loneliness as in the most miserable moment of deserted childhood he never knew. Not a hint, not a shadow of anything outside his consciousness reaches him...

In the midst of the live world he cared for nothing but himself; now in the dead world he is in God's prison, his own separated self. He would not believe in God because he never saw God; now he doubts if there be such a thing as the face of a man—doubts if he ever really saw one, ever anything more than dreamed of such a thing...His fancy will give birth to a thousand fancies, which will run riot like the mice in a house but just deserted...Soon, misery will beget on imagination a thousand shapes of woe, which he will not be able to rule, direct, or even distinguish from real presences—a whole world of miserable contradictions and cold-fever dreams.

But no liveliest human imagination could supply adequate representation of what it would be to be left without a shadow of the presence of God...For the misery would be not merely the absence of all being other than his own self, but the fearful, endless, unavoidable presence of that self. Without the correction, the reflection, the support of other presences, being is not merely unsafe, it is a horror—for anyone but God, who is his own being...It is the lovely creatures God has made all around us, in them giving us himself, that, until we know him, save us from the frenzy of aloneness—for that aloneness is Self, Self, Self. The man who minds only himself must at last go mad if God did not interfere.

Repentance Even In the Black Hell

Can there be any way out of the misery? Will the soul that could not believe in God, with all his lovely world around testifying of him, believe when shut in the prison of its own lonely, weary all-and-nothing? It would for a time try to believe that it was indeed nothing, a mere glow of the setting sun on a cloud of dust, a paltry dream that dreamed itself—then, ah, if only the dream might dream that it was no more! That would be the one thing to hope for. Self-loathing, and that for no sin, from no repentance, from no vision of better, would begin and grow and grow; and to what it might not come no soul can tell—of essential, original misery, uncompromising self-disgust!

Only, then, if a being be capable of self-disgust, is there not some room for hope—as much as a pinch of earth in the cleft of a rock might yield for the growth of a pine? Nay, there must be hope while there is existence; for where there is existence there must be God; and God is for ever good, nor can be other than good.

But alas, the distance from the light! Such a soul is at the farthest verge of life's negation!—no, not the farthest, a man is nearer heaven when in deepest hell than just ere he begins to reap the reward of his doings—for he is in a condition to receive the smallest show of the life that is, as a boon unspeakable.

All his years in the world he received the endless gifts of sun and air, earth and sea and human face divine, as things that came to him because that was their way, and there was no one to prevent them; now the poorest thinning of the darkness he would hail as men of old the glow of a descending angel; it would be as a messenger from God.

Not that he would think of God! It takes long to think of God; but hope, not yet seeming hope, would begin to dawn in his bosom, and the thinner darkness would be as a cave of light, a refuge from the horrid self of which he used to be so proud...

True, all I have been saying is imaginary; but our imagination is made to mirror truth; all the things that appear in it are more or less after the model of things that are; I suspect it is the region whence issues prophecy; and when we are true it will mirror nothing but truth...

And the light would grow and grow across the awful gulf between the soul and its haven—its repentance—for repentance is the first pressure of the bosom of God; and in the twilight, struggling and faint, the man would feel, faint as the twilight, another thought beside his, another thinking Something nigh his dreary self—perhaps the man he had most wronged, most hated, most despised—and would be glad that some one, whoever, was near him: the man he had most injured, and was most ashamed to meet, would be a refuge from himself—oh, how welcome!

So might I imagine a thousand steps up from the darkness, each a little less dark, a little nearer the light—but, ah, the weary way! He cannot come out until he has paid the uttermost farthing!

Repentance once begun, however, may grow more and more rapid! If God once get a willing hold, if with but one finger he touch the man's self, swift as possibility will he draw him from the darkness into the light. For that for which the forlorn, self-ruined wretch was made, was to be a child of God, a partaker of the divine nature, the heir of God and joint heir with Christ. Out of the abyss into which he cast himself, refusing to be the heir of God, he must rise and be raised. To the heart of God, the one and only goal of the human race—the refuge and home of all and each, he must set out and go, or the last glimmer of humanity will die from him.

Whoever will live must cease to be a slave and become a child of God. There is no half-way house of rest, where ungodliness may be dallied with, nor prove quite fatal. Be they few or many cast into such prison as I have endeavoured to imagine, there can be no deliverance for human soul, whether in that prison or out of it, but in paying the last farthing, in becoming lowly, penitent, self-refusing—so receiving the sonship, and learning to cry, *Father!* [36]

And that fire will go searching and burning on in him, as in the highest saint who is not yet pure as he is pure.

But at length, O God, wilt thou not cast Death and Hell into the lake of Fire—even into thine own consuming self? Death shall then die everlastingly, "And Hell itself will pass away, and leave her dolorous mansions to the peering day." Then indeed wilt thou be all in all. For then our poor

---

[36] George MacDonald, *Unspoken Sermons Second Series*, 1885 "The Last Farthing," pp. 107-114 in the Sunrise Centenary Edition, 1995.

brothers and sisters, every one—O God, we trust in thee, the Consuming Fire—shall have been burnt clean and brought home. For if their moans, myriads of ages away, would turn heaven for us into hell—shall a man be more merciful than God? Shall, of all his glories, his mercy alone not be infinite? Shall a brother love a brother more than The Father loves a son?—more than The Brother Christ loves his brother. Would he not die yet again to save one brother more?

As for us, now we will come to thee, our Consuming Fire. And thou wilt not burn us more than we can bear. But thou wilt burn us. And although thou seem to slay us, yet will we trust in thee. [37]

---

[37] George MacDonald, *Unspoken Sermons First Series*, 1867 "The Consuming Fire," pp. 48-49 in the Sunrise Centenary Edition, 1988.

WHAT WE STAND TO LOSE

Frederick Denison Maurice

Nineteenth century English preacher Frederick Denison Maurice (1805-1872) was known in his day by his spoken word. He was one whom George MacDonald always considered a spiritual mentor. The fascinating portrait of the "preacher" in the chapter entitled "A Sunday With Falconer" in MacDonald's David Elginbrod is drawn directly from F.D. Maurice.

Maurice was not only a minister and theologian, but was also trained in law and became one of London's active and outspoken social reformers of the mid 19th century. This made of him a figure of renown and insured that the controversy surrounding his liberal spiritual and social views would be highly public. It is said that his preaching always focused on the fatherhood of God, a fact which obviously drew MacDonald to him.

Thankfully many of Maurice's sermons and several volumes of essays were preserved. The following is taken from the essay quoted in the Introduction, "On Eternal Life And Eternal Death," from Theological Essays. Following the publication of this book in 1853, and with reference to this essay in particular, he was accused of heresy and was forced to resign his professorship of theology at King's College, London.

DID JESUS TEACH US TO FEAR THE FATHER?

However hard and exclusive the Romish Church may have been...it is impossible not to see that she takes up a position which looks, at least, much more comprehensive than that of the Protestant bodies. She assumes the Church to represent mankind...The sacrifice which she presents day by day is declared to be that sacrifice which was made for the sins of the whole world...

We *ought*...to assert the redemption of mankind more distinctly than they do. But it is clear that in practice we do not seem to the world to do so, nor seem to ourselves to do so. The distinctiveness, the individuality, of Protestantism is its strength...But close to that strength is its greatest weakness, that which we all feel, which all in some sort confess, which is the root of our sectarianism, which is continually kept alive by it, and yet which is destroying the very bodies that it has created.

What is the consequence to theology?

The religious men, the saved men, are looked upon as the exceptions to a rule; the world is fallen, outcast, ruined; a few Christians about the signs and tokens of whose Christianity each sect differs, have been rescued from the ruin. I have had to speak in almost every page of this book respecting the habit of mind to which this opinion appertains; and to show how it is at war with all the articles of the Christian faith. I only wish to point out here how it bears upon the subject of everlasting salvation and damnation.

Damnation does not mean what its etymology would lead us to suppose that it means, what it certainly did mean to the Church in former days, amidst all its perplexities and confusions. It is not the loss of a mighty gift which has been bestowed upon the race. Men are not regarded *as rejecting the counsel of God against themselves.* God is represented as the destroyer. Nay, divines go to the length of asserting...that our Lord Himself taught this lesson to His disciples when He said, *And I say unto you, my friends, Be not afraid of them which kill the body, and after that have no more that they can do; but I will forewarn you whom ye shall fear: Fear him, which, after he hath killed, hath power to cast into hell, yea, I say unto you, Fear him. Are not five sparrows sold for two farthings, and not one of them is forgotten before God? But even the very hairs of your head are all numbered. Fear not, therefore; ye are of more value than many sparrows.*

We are come to such a pass as actually to suppose that Christ tells those whom He calls His *friends* not to be afraid of the poor and feeble enemies who can only kill the body, but of that greater enemy who can destroy their very selves, and that this enemy is—not the devil, not the spirit who is going about seeking whom he may devour, not him who was a murderer from the beginning—but that God who cares for the sparrows!

They are to be afraid lest He who numbers the hairs of their head should be plotting their ruin!

Does not this interpretation, which has become so familiar that one hears it without even a hint that there is another, show us on the edge of what an abyss we are standing, how likely we are to confound the Father of lights with the Spirit of darkness?

While this temper of mind continues, it is absolutely inevitable that we should not merely look upon the immense majority of our fellow-creatures as doomed to perdition, but that we should regard the Gospel itself pronouncing their doom. The message which, according to this view of the case, Christ brings from Heaven to earth is, "Your Father has created multitudes whom He means to perish for ever and ever. By my agony and bloody sweat, by my cross and passion, I have induced Him in the case of an inconceivably small minority to forego that design."

Dare we state that proposition to ourselves,—dare we get up into a pulpit and preach it?...

WHY MEN DON'T LISTEN

It is quite clear that the words which go forth from our pulpits on the subject, have no effect at all upon cultivated men of any class, except the effect of making them regard our other utterances with indifference and disbelief....They say that we pronounce a general sentence, and then explain it away in each particular case; they say that we believe that God condemns the world generally, but that, under cover of certain phrases which may mean anything or nothing, we can prove that, on the whole, he rather intends it good than ill. They say that we call upon them to praise Him and give Him thanks, and that what we mean is, that they are to testify emotions towards Him which they do not feel, and which His character, as we represent it, cannot inspire, in order to avert His wrath from them...

The members of the Evangelical Alliance...hear of a vague Universalism being preached from some pulpits in America and on the Continent. They think that notion must encourage sinners to suppose that a certain amount of punishment will be enough to clear off their scores, and to procure them ultimate bliss.

"You are relaxing the strictness of your statements," they say, "just when they need to be more stringent, because all moral obligations are becoming laxer..." Therefore they conclude that such freedom must be checked. It cannot answer, they think, now, however it may have answered heretofore, to leave any loop-hole for doubt about the endless punishment of the wicked.

I have stated the arguments which I think may have inclined worthy and excellent men to arrive at this conclusion; though I believe a more fatal one...cannot be imagined...

Would not...a Gospel of eternal love...present itself to the conscience of men, not as an outrage on their experience, but as the faithful interpreter of it, not as disproving everything that they have dreamed of the willingness of God to save them, but as proving that He is willing and able to save them to the very uttermost?

REMOVE LOVE FROM THE GOSPEL...
AND WE LOSE EVERYTHING

Suppose, instead of taking this method of asserting the truth of all God's words, the most blessed and the most tremendous, we reject the wisdom of our forefathers, and enact an article declaring that all are heretics and deniers of the truth who do not hold that Eternal means endless, and that there cannot be a deliverance from eternal punishment?

What is the consequence?

Simply this, I believe: the whole Gospel of God is set aside.

The state of eternal life and eternal death is not one we can refer only to the future...Every man who knows what it is to have been in a state of sin, knows what it is to have been in a state of death. He cannot connect that death with time; he must say that Christ has brought him out of the bonds of *eternal* death.

Throw that idea into the future, and you deprive it of all its reality, of all its power...It becomes a mere vague dream and shadow...when you project it into a distant world.

And if you take from me the belief that God is always righteous, always maintaining a fight with evil, always seeking to bring His creatures out of it, you take everything from me, all hope now, all hope in the world to come. Atonement, Redemption, Satisfaction, Regeneration, become mere words to which there is no counterpart in reality.

I ask no one to pronounce, for I dare not pronounce myself what are the possibilities of resistance in a human will to the loving will of God. There are times when they seem to me—thinking of myself more than of others—almost infinite.

But I know that there is something which must be infinite. I am obliged to believe in an abyss of love which is deeper than the abyss of death: I dare not lose faith in that love. I sink into death, eternal death if I do. I must feel that this love is compassing the universe. More about it I cannot know. But God knows. I leave myself and all to Him.

It is of this faith that some are seeking to rob us. Have we made up our minds to surrender to it?

Have we resolved that the belief in Endless Punishment shall be not *a* tenet which any one is at liberty to hold...but *the* tenet of the Church to which every other is subordinate...Let us consider, not chiefly what we are accepting, but what we are rejecting, before we tamely submit to this new imposition. [38]

---

[38] F.D. Maurice, *Theological Essays, 1853*, p. 398-406.

ON THE MERITS OF OLD
AND NEW INTERPRETATIONS

A.R. Symonds

In the discussion...some of the things advanced may
seem to the reader novel and startling...Strange as certain
points in the argument may appear, let [the reader] not on
that account refuse carefully to consider them. We are far
too apt to imagine that what to *us* is new, or that differs
from what *we* have been taught or accustomed to believe, is
in itself novel.

But all truth, in relation to men, is new at some time or
other, for it pleases God not to discover all his truth at once,
but to cause it to be revealed in portions. This was his
method in giving those successive revelations, which now,
as a whole, constitute the Bible. Beginning with Genesis, we
trace gradually increasing light till we come to the New
Testament...But even...Jesus Christ did not reveal the whole
truth. 'I have yet many things to say unto you,' He told his
disciples, 'but ye cannot bear them now.' It was reserved for
the Lord the Spirit to lead the Apostles into further
discoveries, and so through them to teach the Church.

With the Apostolic writings we consider the formal
revelations from heaven to be completed. We look for no

more directly inspired writings. But in the *interpretation* of these writings, in the gathering from them what they teach, we do look for advance and development. To possess a completed revelation is one thing, to know all that can be known from that revelation is quite another. In point of fact, the discovery of its *meaning* has been progressive. The Church has not all at once learned all that Holy Scripture reveals, but has advanced, from time to time, in the discernment and understanding of its truths. The profoundest student of the Bible is constrained to confess that there are depths in it he has never fathomed... 'knowledge is come at, by the continuance and progress of learning and liberty, and by particular persons attending to, comparing, and pursuing intimations scattered up and down it, which are overlooked and disregarded by the generality of the world. For this is the way in which all improvements are made, by thoughtful men tracing out obscure hints, as it were, dropped for us...Nor is it at all incredible that a book which has been so long in the possession of mankind should contain many truths as yet undiscovered.'

Nevertheless, when any truth is so brought to light, the hue and cry of novelty is generally raised against it. It conflicts, perhaps, with current beliefs; it fits not in conveniently with what is counted orthodoxy; it is greeted, therefore, with coldness at least, if not hostility...The hope...of the ultimate deliverance of all souls from the power of evil... 'has naturally encountered the suspicions of those Christians whose faith has been crystallized and frozen down in artificial systems of theology. When the doctrines of the gospel have once been compacted together by a logical process, and the result is conceived to embody the whole counsel of God, every new truth drawn fresh from the Scriptures is an unwelcome guest or even a suspected enemy; it wears a strange and foreign aspect, and disturbs the symmetry of a laboriously constructed system.'

As bearing upon this, how interesting is the following prayer of the great and good Dr. Chalmers: 'Deliver me, O Lord, from the narrowing influence of human lessons, from human systems of theology; teach me directly out of the fullness and freeness of thine own Word. Hasten the time when, unfettered by sectarian intolerance, and unawed by the authority of men, the Bible shall make its rightful impression upon all...' And, to quote one more passage, Dr. Goulburn well says: "The truth has a vitality in it still; and many dry rudiments of it, which at present lie dull and uninteresting in our minds, are yet destined to expand and acquire a new significance. Let the mind, then, be frankly open to any and every truth, however unfamiliar to us the first view of it, which may turn out to be in accordance with the teaching of the Apostles."

...a doctrine is by no means to be discarded because it be new. Rather are we to expect that as the labourers diligently dig into the deep mine of Scripture, they will continually be bringing forth from it new ore; that as, in other words, the study of Scripture by pious and searching men advances, so new truths will be elicited, or old truths brought out in such fresh lights as to make them new...

And so I venture to believe that not many years hence will the doctrine of the restitution of all things find general acceptance, and that good men will look back and sadly wonder how they could ever have held the theory which consigns the larger portion of the souls that God made and Christ died for to immutable, irremediable, never-ending torment and perdition...

...an old belief is not necessarily a true one, and...what seems to be a new doctrine is not necessarily an untrue one...as it pleased God, in the first instance, to give his revelation in successive and progressive portions, so has it pleased Him to give the *understanding* of that revelation gradually and progressively; removing former misapprehensions, and causing His Church to see from time to time in his Word what it did not see before." [39]

---

[39] A.R. Symonds, *The Ultimate Reconciliation and Subjection of All Souls to God Under the Kingdom of Christ,* Hamilton, Adams, & Co., London, 1878, pp. 1-4, 8.

On Justice

George MacDonald

What Do We Mean By Justice?

Let us endeavour to see plainly what we mean when we use the word *justice*, and whether we mean what we ought to mean when we use it—especially with reference to God...

What do we oftenest mean by *justice*? Is it not the carrying out of the law, the infliction of penalty assigned to offence? By a just judge we mean a man who administers the law without prejudice...and where guilt is manifest, punishes as much as, and no more than, the law has in the case laid down. It may not be that justice has therefore been done. The law itself may be unjust, and the judge may mistake; or, which is more likely, the working of the law may be foiled by the parasites of the law for their own gain. But even if the law be good, and thoroughly administered, it does not necessarily follow that justice is done.

Suppose my watch has been taken from my pocket; I lay hold of the thief; he is dragged before the magistrate, proved guilty, and sentenced to a just imprisonment: must I walk home satisfied with the result?

Have I had justice done me?

The thief may have had justice done him—but where is my watch? That is gone, and I remain a man wronged.

Who has done me the wrong? The thief.

Who can set the wrong right? The thief, and only the thief; nobody but the man that did the wrong. God may be able to move the man to right the wrong, but God himself cannot right it without the man.

Suppose my watch found and restored, is the account settled between me and the thief? I may forgive him, but is the wrong removed? By no means.

But suppose the thief to bethink himself, to repent. He has, we shall say, put it out of his power to return the watch, but he comes to me and says he is sorry he stole it, and begs me to accept for the present what little he is able to bring, as a beginning of atonement: how should I then regard the matter? Should I not feel that he had gone far to make atonement—done more to make up for the injury he had inflicted upon me, than the mere restoration of the watch, even by himself, could reach to? Would there not lie, in the thief's confession and submission and initial restoration, an appeal to the divinest in me—to the eternal brotherhood? Would it not indeed amount to a sufficing atonement as between man and man? If he offered to bear what I chose to lay upon him, should I feel it necessary, for the sake of justice, to inflict some certain suffering as demanded by righteousness? I should still have a claim upon him for my watch, but should I not be apt to forget it? He who commits the offence can make up for it—and he alone.

One thing must surely be plain—that the punishment of the wrong-doer makes no atonement for the wrong done.

How could it make up to me for the stealing of my watch that the man was punished? The wrong would be there all the same. I am not saying the man ought not to be punished—far from it; I am only saying that the punishment nowise makes up to the man wronged...

Punishment may do good to the man who does the wrong, but that is a thing as different as important.

Another thing plain is, that, even without the material rectification of the wrong where that is impossible, repentance removes the offence which no suffering could. I at least should feel that I had no more quarrel with the man. I should even feel that the gift he had made me, giving into my heart a repentant brother, was infinitely beyond the restitution of what he had taken from me. True, he owed me both himself and the watch, but such a greater does more than include such a less.

If it be objected, "You may forgive, but the man has sinned against God!" —Then...I return, [can] a man be more merciful than his maker!...

There is *no* opposition, *no* strife whatever, between mercy and justice. Those who say justice means the punishing of sin, and mercy the not punishing of sin, and attribute both to God, would make a schism in the very idea of God.

WHAT IS *GOD'S* JUSTICE?

And this brings me to the question, What is meant by divine justice?

Human justice may be a poor distortion of justice, a mere shadow of it; but the justice of God must be perfect...If you ask any ordinary Sunday congregation in England, what is meant by the justice of God, would not nineteen out of twenty answer, that it means the punishing of sin?

Think for a moment what degree of justice it would indicate in a man—that he punished every wrong.

A Roman emperor, a Turkish cadi, might do that, and be the most unjust both of men and judges. Ahab might be just on the throne of punishment, and in his garden the murderer of Naboth.

In God shall we imagine a distinction of office and character?

God is one; and the depth of foolishness is reached by that theology which talks of God as if he held different offices and differed in each. It sets a contradiction in the very nature of God himself. It represents him, for instance, as having to do that as a magistrate which as a father he would not do! The love of the father makes him desire to be unjust as a magistrate!

Oh the folly of any mind that would explain God before obeying him! that would map out the character of God, instead of crying out, Lord, what wouldst thou have me to do?

God is no magistrate; but, if he were, it would be a position to which his fatherhood alone gave him the right; his rights as a father cover every other right he can be analytically supposed to possess.

The justice of God is this, that—to use a boyish phrase...he gives every man, woman, child, and beast, everything that has being, *fair play*; he renders to every man according to his work; and therein lies his perfect mercy; for nothing else could be merciful to the man, and nothing but mercy could be fair to him. God does nothing of which any just man, the thing set fairly and fully before him, so that he understood, would not say, "That is fair."

Who would, I repeat, say a man was a just man because he insisted on prosecuting every offender? A scoundrel might do that....A just man is one who cares, and tries, and always tries, to give fair play to everyone in everything. When we speak of the justice of God, let us see that we do mean justice! Punishment of the guilty may be involved in justice, but it does not constitute the justice of God one atom more than it would constitute the justice of a man...

To say on the authority of the Bible that God does a thing no honourable man would do, is to lie against God; to say that it is therefore right, is to lie against the very spirit of

God. To uphold a lie for God's sake is to be against God, not for him. God cannot be lied for. He is the truth. The truth alone is on his side.

While his child could not see the rectitude of a thing, he would infinitely rather, even if the thing were right, have him say, God could not do that thing, than have him believe that he did it. If the man were sure God did it, the thing he ought to say would be, "Then there must be something about it I do not know, which if I did know, I should see the thing quite differently."

But where an evil thing is invented to explain and account for a good thing, and a lover of God is called upon to believe the invention or be cast out, he needs not mind being cast out, for it is into the company of Jesus. Where there is no ground to believe that God does a thing except that men who would explain God have believed and taught it, he is not a true man who accepts men against his own conscience of God....

I will accept no explanation of any way of God which explanation involves what I should scorn as false and unfair in a man. If you say, That may be right of God to do which it would not be right of man to do, I answer, Yes, because the relation of the maker to his creatures is very different from the relation of one of those creatures to another...he can have no duty that is both just and merciful. More is required of the maker, by his own act of creation, than can be required of men. More and higher justice and righteousness is required of him...greater nobleness, more penetrating sympathy; and *nothing* but what, if an honest man understood it, he would say was right...God may do what seems to a man not right, but it must so seem to him because God works on higher, on divine, on perfect principles, too right for a selfish, unfair, or unloving man to understand. But least of all must we accept some low notion of justice in a man, and argue that God is just in doing after that notion.

THE RELATIONSHIP BETWEEN SIN AND PUNISHMENT

The common idea, then, is that the justice of God consists in punishing sin: it is in the hope of giving a larger idea of the justice of God in punishing sin that I ask, "Why is God bound to punish sin?"

"How could he be a just God and not punish sin?"

"Mercy is a good and right thing," I answer, "and but for sin there could be no mercy. We are enjoined to forgive, to be merciful, to be as our father in heaven. Two rights cannot possibly be opposed to each other. If God punish sin, it must be merciful to punish sin; and if God forgive sin, it must be just to forgive sin. We are required to forgive, with the argument that our father forgives. It must, I say, be right to forgive. Every attribute of God must be infinite as himself. He cannot be sometimes merciful, and not always merciful. He cannot be just, and not always just. Mercy belongs to him, and needs no contrivance of theologic chicanery to justify it."

"Then you mean that it is wrong to punish sin, therefore God does not punish sin?"

"By no means; God does punish sin, but there is no opposition between punishment and forgiveness. The one may be essential to the possibility of the other. *Why*, I repeat, does God punish sin? That is my point."

"Because in itself sin deserves punishment."

"Then how can he tell us to forgive it?"

"He punishes, and having punished he forgives."

"That will hardly do. If sin demands punishment, and the righteous punishment is given, then the man is free. Why should he be forgiven?"

"He needs forgiveness because no amount of punishment will meet his deserts."

I avoid for the present, as anyone may perceive, the probable expansion of this reply...and this brings me to the fault in the whole idea.

Punishment is *nowise* an *offset* to sin.

Foolish people sometimes, in a tone of self-gratulatory pity, will say, "If I have sinned I have suffered." Yes, verily, but what of it? What merit is there in it...what did that do to make up for the wrong? That you may have been bettered by your suffering is well for you, but what atonement is there in the suffering? The notion is a false one altogether.

Punishment, deserved suffering, is no equipoise to sin. It is no use laying it on the other scale. It will not move it a hair's breadth. Suffering weights nothing at all against sin...If it were an offset to wrong, then God would be bound to punish for the sake of punishment; but he cannot be, for he forgives. Then it is not for the sake of the punishment, as a thing that in itself ought to be done, but for the sake of something else, as a means to an end, that God punishes....

Primarily, God is not bound to *punish* sin; he is bound to *destroy* sin.

If he were not the Maker, he might not be bound to destroy sin—I do not know; but seeing he has created creatures who have sinned, and therefore sin has, by the creating act of God, come into the world, God is, in his own righteousness, bound to destroy sin.

"But that is to have no mercy."

You mistake. God does destroy sin; he is always destroying sin. In him I trust that he is destroying sin in me. He is always saving the sinner from his sin and that is destroying sin. But vengeance on the sinner, the law of a tooth for a tooth, is not in the heart of God, neither in his hand. If the sinner and the sin in him, are the concrete object of the divine wrath, then indeed there can be no mercy. Then indeed there will be an end put to sin by the destruction of the sin and the sinner together. But thus would no atonement be wrought—nothing be done to make up for the wrong God has allowed to come into being by creating man. There must be an atonement, a making-up, a bringing together—an atonement which, I say, cannot be made except by the man who has sinned.

Punishment, I repeat, is not the thing required of God, but the absolute destruction of sin.

What better is the world, what better is the sinner, what better is God, what better is the truth, that the sinner should suffer—continue suffering to all eternity? Would there be less sin in the universe? Would there be a making-up for sin? Would it show God justified in doing what he knew would bring sin into the world, justified in making creatures who he knew would sin? What setting-right would come of the sinner's suffering? If justice demand it, if suffering be the equivalent for sin, then the sinner must suffer, then God is bound to exact his suffering, and not pardon; and so the making of man was a tyrannical deed, a creative cruelty. But grant that the sinner has deserved to suffer, no amount of suffering is any atonement for his sin. To suffer to all eternity could not make up for one unjust word.

Does that mean, then, that for an unjust word I deserve to suffer to all eternity? The unjust word is an eternally evil thing; nothing but God in my heart can cleanse me from the evil that uttered it; but does it follow that I saw the evil of what I did so perfectly, that eternal punishment for it would be just? Sorrow and confession and self-abasing love will make up for the evil word; suffering will not....

The only vengeance worth having on sin is to make the sinner himself its executioner.

Sin and punishment are in no antagonism to each other in man, any more than pardon and punishment are in God...Sin and suffering are not natural opposites; the opposite of evil is good, not suffering; the opposite of sin is not suffering, but righteousness.

The path across the gulf that divides right from wrong is not the fire, but repentance. If my friend has wronged me, will it console me to see him punished?...Will his agony be a balm to my deep wound?...But would not the shadow of repentant grief, the light of reviving love on his countenance, heal it at once however deep?

Take any of those wicked people in Dante's hell, and ask wherein is justice served by their punishment? Mind, I am not saying it is not right to punish them; I am saying that justice is not, never can be, satisfied by suffering...Such justice as Dante's keeps wickedness alive in its most terrible forms...All hell cannot make Vanni Fucci say "I was wrong." God is triumphantly defeated, I say, throughout the hell of his vengeance. Although against evil, it is but the vain and wasted cruelty of a tyrant. There is no destruction of evil thereby, but an enhancing of its horrible power in the midst of the most agonizing and disgusting tortures a *divine* imagination can invent...but while I regard the smallest sin as infinitely loathsome, I do not believe that any being, never good enough to see the essential ugliness of sin, could sin so as to *deserve* such punishment.

I am not now, however, dealing with the question of the duration of punishment, but with the idea of punishment itself; and would only say in passing, that the notion that a creature born imperfect, nay, born with impulses to evil not of his own generating, and which he could not help having, a creature to whom the true face of God was never presented, and by whom it never could have been seen, should be thus condemned, is as loathsome a lie against God as could find place in heart too undeveloped to understand what justice is, and too low to look up into the face of Jesus. It never in truth found place in any heart, though in many a pettifogging brain. There is but one thing lower than deliberately to believe a lie, and that is to worship the God of whom it is believed....

TRUE JUSTICE AND ATONEMENT

When a man loathes himself, he has begun to be saved. Punishment tends to this result.

Not for its own sake, not as a make-up for sin, not for divine revenge—horrible word, not for any satisfaction to justice, can punishment exist.

Punishment is for the sake of amendment and atonement. God is bound by his love to punish sin in order to deliver his creature; he is bound by his justice to destroy sin in his creation.

Love is justice—is the fulfilling of the law, for God as well as for his children.

This is the reason of punishment; this is why justice requires that the wicked shall not go unpunished—that they, through the eye-opening power of pain, may come to see and do justice, may be brought to desire and make all possible amends, and so become just. Such punishment concerns justice in the deepest degree. For Justice, that is God, is bound in himself to see justice done by his children—not in the mere outward act, but in their very being. He is bound in himself to make up for wrong done by his children, and he can do nothing to make up for the wrong done but by bringing about the repentance of the wrongdoer.

When the man says, "I did wrong; I hate myself and my deed; I cannot endure to think that I did it!" then, I say, is atonement begun. Without that, all that the Lord did would be lost. He would have made no atonement. Repentance, restitution, confession, prayer for forgiveness, righteous dealing thereafter, is the sole possible, the only true make-up for sin. For nothing less than this did Christ die. When a man acknowledges the right he denied before; when he says to the wrong, "I abjure you; I loathe you; I see now what you are; I could not see it before because I would not;

God forgive me; make me clean, or let me die!" then justice, that is God, has conquered—and not till then.

"What atonement is there?"

Every atonement that God cares for; and the work of Jesus Christ on earth was the creative atonement because it works atonement in every heart. He brings and is bringing God and man, and man and man, into perfect unity...

"That is dangerous doctrine!"

More dangerous than you think to many things—to every evil, to every lie, and among the rest to every false trust in what Christ did, instead of in Christ himself. Paul glories in the cross of Christ, but he does not trust in the cross: he trusts in the living Christ and his living father.

Justice then requires that sin should be put an end to; and not that only, but that it should be atoned for; and where punishment can do anything to this end, where it can help the sinner to know what he has been guilty of, where it can soften his heart to see his pride and wrong and cruelty, justice requires that punishment shall not be spared. And the more we believe in God, the surer we shall be that he will spare nothing that suffering can do to deliver his child from death. If suffering cannot serve this end, we need look for no more hell, but for the destruction of sin by the destruction of the sinner. That, however, would, it appears to me, be for God to suffer defeat, blameless indeed, but defeat.

If God be defeated, he must destroy—that is, he must withdraw life. How can he go on sending forth his life into irreclaimable souls, to keep sin alive in them throughout the ages of eternity? But then, I say, no atonement would be made for the wrongs they have done; God remains defeated, for he has created that which sinned, and which would not repent and make up for its sin.

But those who believe that God will thus be defeated by many souls, must surely be of those who do not believe he cares enough to do his very best for them. He *is* their Father, he had power to make them out of himself, separate from himself, and capable of being one with him: surely he will somehow save and keep them. Not the power of sin itself can close *all* the channels between creating and created.

WHY WE ENJOY SEEING SIN PUNISHED

The notion of suffering as an offset for sin, the foolish idea that man by suffering borne may get out from under the hostile claim to which his wrong-doing has subjected him, comes first of all, I think, from the satisfaction we feel when wrong comes to grief.

Why do we feel this satisfaction?

Because we hate wrong, but, not being righteous ourselves, more or less hate the wronger as well as his wrong, hence are not only righteously pleased to behold law's disapproval proclaimed in his punishment, but unrighteously pleased with his suffering, because of the impact upon us of his wrong. In this way the inborn justice of our nature passes over to evil. It is no pleasure to God, as it so often is to us, to see the wicked suffer. To regard any suffering with satisfaction, save it be sympathetically with its curative quality, comes of evil, is inhuman because it is undivine, is a thing God is incapable of.

His nature is always to forgive, and just because he forgives, he punishes.

Because God is so altogether alien to wrong, because it is to him a heart-pain and trouble that one of his little ones should do the evil thing, there is, I believe, no extreme of suffering to which, for the sake of destroying the evil thing in them, he would not subject them. A man might flatter, or bribe, or coax a tyrant; but there is no refuge from the love of God; that love will, for very love, insist upon the uttermost farthing.

"That is not the sort of love I care about!"

No; how should you?...You cannot care for it until you begin to know it. But the eternal love will not be moved to yield you to the selfishness that is killing you...You may sneer at such a love, but the Son of God who took the weight of that love, and bore it through the whole world, is content with it, and so is everyone who knows it.

The love of the Father is a radiant perfection. Love and not self-love is lord of the universe. Justice demands your punishment, because justice demands, and will have, the destruction of sin. Justice demands your punishment because it demands that your father should do his best for you...

The notion that the salvation of Jesus is a salvation from the consequences of our sins, is a false, mean, low notion. The salvation of Christ is salvation from the smallest tendency or leaning to sin. It is a deliverance into the pure air of God's ways of thinking and feeling. It is a salvation that makes the heart pure, with the will and choice of the heart to be pure. To such a heart, sin is disgusting...No soul is saved that would not prefer hell to sin. Jesus did not die to save us from punishment; he was called Jesus because he should save his people from their sins.

THE EFFECT ON POPULAR THEOLOGY

If punishment be no atonement, how does the fact bear on the popular theology...? Most of us have been more or less trained in it, and not a few of us have thereby, thank God, learned what it is—an evil thing, to be cast out of intellect and heart. Many imagine it dead and gone, but in reality it lies at root...of much the greater part of the teaching of Christianity in the country; and is believed in—so far as the false *can* be believed in—by many who think they have left it behind, when they have merely omitted the truest, most offensive modes of expressing its doctrines. It is humiliating to find how many comparatively honest people think they get rid of a falsehood by softening the statement of it...

I have passed through no change of opinion concerning it since first I began to write and speak; but I have written little and spoken less about it, because I would preach no mere negation. My work was not to destroy the false, except as it came in the way of building the true. Therefore I sought to speak but what I believed, saying little concerning what I did not believe; trusting, as now I trust, in the true to cast out the false, and shunning dispute. Neither will I now enter any theological lists to be the champion for or against mere doctrine. I have no desire to change the opinion of man or woman. Let everyone for me hold what he pleases...let the Lord himself teach them...

A man who has not the mind of Christ—and no man has the mind of Christ except him who makes it his business to obey him—cannot have correct opinions concerning him...

Our business is not to think correctly, but to live truly; then first will there be a possibility of our thinking correctly. One chief cause of the amount of unbelief in the world is, that those who have seen something of the glory of Christ, set themselves to theorize concerning him rather than to obey him. In teaching men, they have not taught them Christ, but taught them about Christ. More eager after credible theory than after doing the truth, they have speculated in a condition of heart in which it was impossible they should understand; they have presumed to explain a Christ whom years and years of obedience could alone have made them able to comprehend. Their teaching of him, therefore, has been repugnant to the common sense of many who had not half their privileges, but in whom as in Nathanael, there was no guile.

Such, naturally, press their theories, in general derived from them of old time, upon others, insisting on their thinking about Christ as they think, instead of urging them to go to Christ to be taught by him whatever he chooses to teach them. They do their unintentional worst to stop all growth, all life.

From such and their false teaching I would gladly help to deliver the true-hearted. Let the dead bury their dead, but I would do what I can to keep them from burying the living.

WHAT ABOUT CHRIST'S SUFFERING FOR MAN'S SIN?

If there be no satisfaction to justice in the mere punishment of the wrong-doer, what shall we say of the notion of satisfying justice by causing one to suffer who is not the wrong-doer?

And what, moreover, shall we say to the notion that, just because he is not the person who deserves to be punished, but is absolutely innocent, his suffering gives perfect satisfaction to the perfect justice?...it is no more punishment, but mere suffering the law requires!

The thing gets worse and worse. I declare my utter and absolute repudiation of the idea in any form whatever...

What! God, the father of Jesus Christ, like that! His justice contented with direct injustice! The anger of him who will nowise clear the guilty, appeased by the suffering of the innocent!

Very God forbid!

Observe: the evil fancy actually substitutes for punishment not mere suffering, but that suffering which is farthest from punishment; and this when, as I have shown, punishment, the severest, can be no satisfaction to justice!

How did it come ever to be imagined? It sprang from the trustless dread that cannot believe in the forgiveness of the Father; cannot believe that even God will do anything for them; cannot trust him without a legal arrangement to bind him.

How many, failing to trust God, fall back on *a text,* as they call it! It sprang from the pride that will understand what it cannot, before it will obey what it sees...

If anyone say, "But I believe what you despise," I answer,

To believe it is your punishment for being able to believe it; you may call it your reward, if you will. You ought not to be able to believe it. It is the merest, poorest, most shameless fiction, invented without the perception that it was an invention—fit to satisfy the intellect, doubtless, of the inventor, else he could not have invented it. It has seemed to satisfy also many a humble soul, content to take what was given, and not think; content that another should think for him, and tell him what was in the mind of his Father in heaven.

Again I say, let the person who can be so satisfied be so satisfied...That he can be content with it, argues him unready to receive better. So long as he can believe false things concerning God, he is such as is capable of believing them—with how much or how little of blame, God knows. Opinion, right or wrong, will do nothing to save him. I would that he thought no more about this or any other opinion, but set himself to do the work of the Master. With his opinions, true or false, I have nothing to do.

It is because such as he force evil things upon their fellows—utter or imply them from the seat of authority or influence...that I have any right to speak. I would save my fellows from having what notion of God is possible to them blotted out by a lie.

If it be asked how, if it be false, the doctrine of substitution can have been permitted to remain so long an article of faith to so many, I answer, On the same principle on which God took up and made use of the sacrifices men had, in their lack of faith, invented as a way of pleasing him...God accepted men's sacrifices until he could get them to see—and with how many has he yet not succeeded, in the church and out of it!—that he does not care for such things.

How Can A False Teaching Strike Such Deep Root?

"But," again it may well be asked, "whence then has sprung the undeniable potency of that teaching?"

I answer, From its having in it a notion of God and his Christ, poor indeed and faint, but, by the very poverty and untruth in its presentation, fitted to the weakness and unbelief of men, seeing it was by men invented to meet and ease the demand made upon their own weakness and unbelief.

Thus the leaven spreads.

The truth is there. It is Christ the glory of God. But the ideas that poor slavish souls breed concerning this glory the moment the darkness begins to disperse, is quite another thing.

Truth is indeed too good for men to believe; they must dilute it before they can take it; they must dilute it before they dare give it. They must make it less true before they can believe it enough to get any good of it.

Unable to believe in the love of the Lord Jesus Christ, they invented a mediator in his mother, and so were able to approach a little where else they had stood away; unable to believe in the forgiveness of their father in heaven, they invented a way to be forgiven that should not demand of him so much; which might make it right for him to forgive; which should save them from having to believe downright in the tenderness of his father-heart, for that they found impossible.

They thought him bound to punish for the sake of punishing, as an offset to their sin; they could not believe in clear forgiveness; that did not seem divine; it needed to be justified; so they invented for its justification a horrible injustice, involving all that was bad in sacrifice, even human sacrifice. They invented a satisfaction for sin which was an insult to God.

He sought no satisfaction, but an obedient return to the Father. What satisfaction was needed he made himself in what he did to cause them to turn from evil and go back to him.

The thing was too simple for complicated unbelief and the arguing spirit.

Gladly would I help their followers to loathe such thoughts of God; but for that, they themselves must grow better men and women. While they are capable of being satisfied with them, there would be no advantage in their becoming intellectually convinced that such thoughts were wrong. I would not speak a word to persuade them of it. Success would be worthless. They would but remain what they were—children capable of thinking meanly of their father.

When the heart recoils, discovering how horrible it would be to have such an unreality for God, it will begin to search about and see whether it must indeed accept such statements concerning God; it will search after a real God by whom to hold fast, a real God to deliver them from the terrible idol.

It is for those thus moved that I write, not at all for the sake of disputing with those who love the lie they may not be to blame for holding...

THE CORE OF THE EVANGELICAL TRADITION OF THE ELDERS

Instead of giving their energy to do the will of God, men of power have given it to the construction of a system by which to explain why Christ must die, what were the necessities and designs of God in permitting his death; and men of power of our own day, while casting from them not a little of the good in the teaching of the Roman Church, have clung to the morally and spiritually vulgar idea of a justice and satisfaction held by pagan Rome, buttressed by the Jewish notion of sacrifice...Better the reformers had kept their belief in a purgatory, and parted with what is called vicarious sacrifice!

Their system is briefly this: God is bound to punish sin, and to punish it to the uttermost. His justice requires that sin be punished. But he loves man, and does not want to punish him if he can help it. Jesus Christ says, "I will take his punishment upon me." God accepts his offer, and lets man go unpunished—upon a condition. His justice is more than satisfied by the punishment of an infinite being instead of a world of worthless creatures. The suffering of Jesus is of greater value than that of all the generations, through endless ages, because he is infinite, pure, perfect in love and truth, being God's own everlasting son.

God's condition with man is, that he believe in Christ's atonement thus explained. A man must say, "I have sinned, and deserve to be tortured to all eternity. But Christ has paid my debts, by being punished instead of me. Therefore he is my Saviour. I am now bound by gratitude to him to turn away from evil." Some would doubtless insist on his saying a good deal more, but this is enough for my purpose....

Strange that in a Christian land it should need to be said, that to punish the innocent and let the guilty go free is unjust! It wrongs the innocent, the guilty, and God himself. It would be the worst of all wrongs to the guilty to treat them as innocent. The whole device is a piece of spiritual charlatanry...If the wicked ought to be punished, it were the worst possible perversion of justice to take a righteous being however strong, and punish him instead of the sinner however weak....

If you say it is justice, not God that demands the suffering, I say justice cannot demand that which is unjust, and the whole thing is unjust. God is absolutely just, and there is no deliverance from his justice, which is one with his mercy. The device is an absurdity—a grotesquely deformed absurdity. To represent the living God as a party to such a style of action, is to veil with a mask of cruelty and hypocrisy the face whose glory can be seen only in the face of Jesus...this is not our God! This is not he for whom we have waited!...

I will not have the God of the scribes and the pharisees whether Jewish or Christian, protestant, Roman, or Greek, but thy father, O Christ! He is my God....

To believe in a vicarious sacrifice, is to think to take refuge with the Son from the righteousness of the Father; to take refuge with his work instead of with the Son himself; to take refuge with a theory of that work instead of the work itself; to shelter behind a false quirk of law instead of nestling in the eternal heart of the unchangeable and righteous Father, who is merciful in that he renders to every man according to his work, and compels their obedience, nor admits judicial quibble or subterfuge.

God will never let a man off with any fault. He must have him clean. He will excuse him to the very uttermost of truth, but not a hair's-breadth beyond it; he is his true father, and will have his child true as his son Jesus Christ is true...He is God beyond all that heart hungriest for love and righteousness could to eternity desire.

BUT MANY GOOD PEOPLE BELIEVE IT

If you say the best of men have held the opinions I stigmatize, I answer, "Some of the best of men have indeed held these theories, and...I have loved and honoured some heartily and humbly—but because of what they *were*, not because of what they *thought*; and they were what they were in virtue of their obedient faith, not their opinion...In virtue of knowing God by obeying his son, they rose above the theories they had never looked in the face, and so had never recognized as evil...."

There is nothing for any lie but the pit of hell. Yet until the man sees the thing to be a lie, how shall he but hold it! Are there not mingled with it shadows of the best truth in the universe? So long as a man is able to love a lie, he is incapable of seeing it is a lie. He who is true, out and out, will know at once an untruth; and to that vision we must all come.

I do not write for the sake of those who either make or heartily accept any lie. When they see the glory of God, they will see the eternal difference between the false and the true, and not till then. I write for those whom such teaching as theirs has folded in a cloud through which they cannot see the stars of heaven, so that some of them even doubt if there be any stars in heaven.

For the holy ones who believed and taught these things in days gone by, all is well. Many of the holiest of them cast the lies from them long ere the present teachers of them were born. Many who would never have invented them for themselves, yet receiving them with the seals affixed of so many good men, took them in their humility as recognized truths...and, oppressed by authority...did not dare dispute them, but proceeded to order their lives by what truths they found in their company, and so had their reward, the reward of obedience, in being by that obedience brought to know God, which knowledge broke for them the net of a presumptuous self-styled orthodoxy.

Every man who tries to obey the Master is my brother, whether he counts me such or not, and I revere him; but dare I give quarter to what I see to be a lie, because my brother believes it? The lie is not of God, whoever may hold it.

"Well, then," will many say, "If you thus unceremoniously cast to the winds the doctrine of vicarious sacrifice, what theory do you propose to substitute in its stead?"

"In the name of truth," I answer, *None*. I will send out no theory of mine to rouse afresh little whirlwinds of dialogistic dust mixed with dirt and straws and holy words, hiding the Master in talk about him...

"Will you then take from me my faith, and help me to no other?"

Your faith! God forbid. Your theory is not your faith, nor anything like it. Your faith is your obedience; your theory I know not what...Trust in God. Obey the word—every word of the Master. That is faith; and so believing, your opinion will grow out of your true life, and be worthy of it. Peter says the Lord gives the spirit to them that obey him; the spirit of the Master, and that alone, can guide you to any theory that it will be of use to you to hold. A theory arrived-at any other way is not worth the time spent on it...

To put off obeying him till we find a credible theory concerning him, is to set aside the potion we know it our duty to drink, for the study of the various schools of therapy.

You know what Christ requires of you is right—much of it at least you believe to be right, and your duty to do, whether he said it or not: *do it*...Obey the truth, I say, and let theory wait. Theory may spring from life, but never life from theory.

I Believe!

I will not then tell you what I think, but I will tell any man who cares to hear it what I believe....

I believe in Jesus Christ, the eternal Son of God, my elder brother, my lord and master; I believe that he has a right to my absolute obedience...that to obey him is to ascend the pinnacle of my being...

I believe that he died that I might die like him—die to any ruling power in me but the will of God...

I believe that he is my Saviour from myself, and from all that has come of loving myself, from all that God does not love, and would not have me love...that he died that the justice, the mercy of God, might have its way with me, making me just as God is just, merciful as he is merciful, perfect as my father in heaven is perfect.

I believe and pray that he will give me what punishment I need to set me right, or keep me from going wrong. I believe that he died to save me from all meanness, all pretence, all falseness, all unfairness, all poverty of spirit, all cowardice, all fear, all anxiety, all forms of self-love, all trust or hope in possession; to make me merry as a child, the child of our father in heaven, loving nothing but what is lovely, desiring nothing I should be ashamed to let the universe of God see me desire.

I believe that God is just like Jesus, only greater yet, for Jesus said so. I believe that God is absolutely, grandly beautiful, even as the highest soul of man counts beauty, but infinitely beyond that soul's highest idea—with the beauty that creates beauty, not merely shows it, or itself exists beautiful.

I believe that God has always done, is always doing his best for every man; that no man is miserable because God is forgetting him; that he is not a God to crouch before, but our father, to whom the child-heart cries exultant, "Do with me as thou wilt."

I believe that there is nothing good for me or for any man but God, and more and more of God, and that alone through knowing Christ can we come nigh to him.

I believe that no man is ever condemned for any sin except one—that he will not leave his sins and come out of them, and be the child of him who is his father.

I believe that justice and mercy are simply one and the same thing; without justice to the full there can be no mercy, and without mercy to the full there can be no justice; that such is the mercy of God that he will hold his children in the consuming fire of his distance until they pay the uttermost farthing, until they drop the purse of selfishness with all the dross that is in it, and rush home to the Father and the Son, and the many brethren—rush inside the centre of the life-giving fire whose outer circles burn.

I believe that no hell will be lacking which would help the just mercy of God to redeem his children.

I believe that to him who obeys, and thus opens the doors of his heart to receive the eternal gift, God gives the spirit of his son, the spirit of himself, to be in him, and lead him to the understanding of all truth; that the true disciple shall thus always know what he ought to do, though not necessarily what another ought to do; that the spirit of the father and the son enlightens by teaching righteousness.

I believe that no teacher should strive to make men think as he thinks, but to lead them to the living Truth, to the Master himself, of whom alone they can learn anything, who will make them in themselves know what is true by the very seeing of it. I believe that the inspiration of the Almighty alone gives understanding. I believe that to be the disciple of Christ is the end of being; that to persuade men to be his disciples is the end of teaching.

"The sum of all this is that you do not believe in the atonement?"

I believe in Jesus Christ.

Nowhere am I requested to believe *in* any thing, or *in* any statement, but everywhere to believe in God and in Jesus Christ.

In what you call *the atonement*, in what you mean by the word, what I have already written must make it plain enough I do not believe. God forbid I should, for it would be to believe a lie, and a lie which is to blame for much non-acceptance of the gospel in this and other lands.

But, as the word was used by the best English writers at the time when the translation of the Bible was made—with all my heart, and soul, and strength, and mind, I believe in the atonement, call it the *a-tone-ment,* or the *at-one-ment,* as you please. I believe that Jesus Christ *is* our atonement; that through him we are reconciled to, made one with God....

I am not writing, neither desire to write, a treatise on the atonement; my business being to persuade men to be atoned to God...but I will go so far to meet my questioner as to say...that, even in the sense of the atonement being a making-up for the evil done by men toward God, I believe in the atonement.

Did not the Lord cast himself into the eternal gulf of evil yawning between the children and the Father? Did he not bring the Father to us, let us look on our eternal Sire in the face of his true son, that we might have that in our hearts which alone could make us love him—a true sight of him? Did he not insist on the one truth of the universe, the one saving truth, that God was just what he was?...Did he not thus lay down his life persuading us to lay down ours at the feet of the Father? Has not his very life by which he died passed into those who have received him, and re-created theirs, so that now they live with the life which alone is life? Did he not foil and slay evil by letting all the waves and billows of its horrid sea break upon him, go over him, and die without rebound—spend their rage, fall defeated, and cease?

Verily, he made atonement!...

God...sacrificed his own son to us; there was no way else of getting the gift of himself into our hearts. Jesus sacrificed himself to his father and the children to bring them together...how can I but believe in the atonement of Jesus Christ? I believe it heartily, as God means it....

Who is the mover, the causer, the persuader, the creator of the repentance of the passion that restores fourfold?— Jesus, our propitiation, our atonement...

He is my life, my joy, my lord, my owner, the perfecter of my being by the perfection of his own. I dare not say with Paul that I am the slave of Christ; but my highest aspiration and desire is to be the slave of Christ. [40]

[40] George MacDonald, *Unspoken Sermons Third Series,* 1889, "Justice," pp. 110-159 in the Sunrise Centenary Edition, 1996.

AION, AIONIOS, AND KOLASIS

Jukes, Allin, Symonds, Vine, and Barclay

Italics have been added to the originals for emphasis.

Andrew Jukes asserts:

"...the language of the New Testament, in its use of the word which our Translators have rendered 'for ever' and 'for ever and ever,' [αιωνιου] but which is literally 'for the age,' or 'for the ages of ages,' points not uncertainly to the same solution of the great riddle, though as yet the glad tidings of the 'ages to come' have been but little opened out...At any rate, and whatever the future 'ages' may be, those past...are clearly *not endless*; and the language of Scripture as to those to come seems to teach that they are *limited*...Would it not have been better therefore, and more respectful to the Word of God, had our Translators been content in every place to give the exact meaning of the words, which they render 'for ever,' or 'for ever and ever,' but which are simply 'for the age,' or 'for the ages of ages'...But even more remarkable are the words, in St. Peter's Second Epistle, which our Version translates 'for ever,' but which are literally 'for the day of the age'...These and other similar forms of expression cannot have been used without a purpose. It is, therefore, a matter of regret that our Translators should not have rendered them exactly and literally; for surely the words which Divine Wisdom has chosen must have a reason, even where readers and translators lack the light to apprehend it." [41]

Jukes' view is echoed by Thomas Allin:

"Let us consider the true meaning of the words *aion* and *aionios*. These are the originals of the terms rendered by our translators 'everlasting,' 'for ever and ever': and on this translation, so misleading, a vast portion of the popular dogma of endless torment is built up. I say, without hesitation, misleading and incorrect; for *aion* means 'an age,' a limited period, whether long or short, though often of indefinite length; and the adjective *aionios* means 'of the age,' 'age-long,' 'æonian,' and *never* 'everlasting.'" [42]

In the case of the Greek $\alpha\iota\omega\upsilon$, or aion meaning *age*, W.E. Vine clarifies:

"Aion ($\alpha\iota\omega\upsilon$,), an age, is translated 'eternal'..." [43]

---

[41] Andrew Jukes, *The Restitution of All Things*, 1867, pp. 57, 61-3.

[42] Thomas Allin, *Christ Triumphant*, 1890, p. 258.

[43] W.E. Vine, *Vine's Expository Dictionary of New Testament Words*, Fleming Hr. Revell, 1940.

Referring to the punishment (κολασιν, *kolasin*) of Matthew 25:46, William Barclay emphasizes:

"...there is *no* instance in Greek where *kolasis* does not mean remedial punishment. This would enable us to argue that God's punishment is *always* for man's cure...It is the simple fact that in Greek *kolasis always* means a remedial punishment." [44]

And A.R. Symonds adds:

"And if the Greek word rendered 'everlasting' in the English version does not support the notion of endless suffering, much less does the word which is translated 'punishment.' The distinctive meaning of this word, κολασιζ, is *corrective* punishment, being derived from a verb which means to prune. I say its distinctive meaning is this, in relation to another word, τιμωρια, which signifies vindictive punishment. In τιμωρια the vindictive character of the punishment is the predominant through; it is the Latin ultio, vengeance, punishment as satisfying the inflictor's sense of outraged justice, as defending his own honour and that of violated law. In κολασιζ, on the other hand, it is more the notion of punishment as it has reference to the correction and bettering of him that endures it; it is castigatio, chastisement, and has naturally for the most part a milder use than τιμωρια." [45]

---

[44] William Barclay, Letter to Michael Phillips, September 26, 1973

[45] A.R. Symonds, *The Ultimate Reconciliation and Subjection of All Souls to God Under the Kingdom of Christ*, Hamilton, Adams, & Co., London, 1878, p. 130-131.

ON AEONIAL LIFE

A.P. Adams

During the latter third of the 19th century, especially in England, interest in the doctrine of universal reconciliation positively exploded within the Christian church, leading to dozens if not hundreds of ministers and authors preaching and writing on the subject. George MacDonald, F.D. Maurice, Andrew Jukes, Thomas Allin, and Edna Lyall were but a handful in a groundswell of men and women whose writings attempted to shine new scriptural light on God's eternal purposes. Along with A.E. Knock and others, A.P. Adams (1847-1925) was one of the pioneers who stood at the vanguard of this movement in America. As a young Methodist minister in Massachusetts, Adams heard a message on universal reconciliation and became convinced of the truth of the doctrine. Introducing it to his own congregation, he went on to write a number of pamphlets and books on the subject, including The True Basis of Redemption and Bible Harmony. He also published a newsletter called "The Spirit of the Word. Predictably, Adams was brought before his denomination on charges of heresy. He was expelled and his ordination revoked. In the 20th century, the works of Adams were revived and republished largely through the efforts of George Hawtin.

There are several different words in the original New Testament that are translated in the common version by this one English word, world; the two principle ones are *aeon* and *kosmos*. Though both of these words are usually rendered world, yet they are really very distinct and different in their meaning and ought to have been rendered respectively age and world. We shall have space here for the consideration of only the former word, aeon, i.e. age...

There are only two places in the common version where the word *aeon* is rendered, as it should be in every case, age; but these two instances are significant, because they show of themselves the meaning of the word. In Col. 1:26 we read of "the mystery which hath been hid from *ages* and from generations but now is made manifest to His saints." In Eph. 2:7 we read that "in the ages to come God will show the exceeding riches of His grace". Now these passages plainly indicate two things in regard to this word. (1) *The ages are limited by periods of time.* Several of them have run their course and come to an end in the past, and there are yet more to come. (2) *The "ages to come" are to be richer in the manifestation of the grace of God than the present or past ages.* In other words it appears that God's grace broadens and His plan develops as the ages roll, mysteries that have been hid in past ages are made known, and the future ages are to witness the "riches of His grace" to an extent "exceeding" that of any previous age.

This word aeon occurs in the New Testament in so many peculiar and varying forms as to make it certain that it expresses some deep and important meaning well worth searching out. First we have the simple word many times repeated, both in the singular and plural. Then we have the word in combination with several prepositions: *from* the age, Luke 1:7; *from* the ages, Eph. 3:9; *out of the* age, John 9:32; *before* the ages, 1 Cor. 2:7; *before* times of ages or *before* age-times, Tim. 1:2; *the purpose of* the ages, Eph. 3:11 (N.V. margin); *the age to come,* Heb. 6:5; *the ages to come,* Eph. 2:7; *the end of* the age, Matt. 24:3; *the end* of the ages, Heb. 9:26; *the ends* of the ages, 1 Cor. 10:11. Furthermore in connection with the preposition *unto* we find the following remarkable changes:

1. Unto the age. Mark 3:29
2. Unto the ages. Luke 1:33
3. Unto all the ages. Jude 25
4. Unto the age of the age. Heb. 1:8
5. Unto all the generations of the age of the ages. Eph. 3:21
6. Unto the ages of the ages. Rev. 1:6
7. Unto the day of an age. 2 Pet. 3:18

Can anyone suppose that these peculiar forms have no special meaning? Is all this a mere play upon words? Simply purposeless repetition?...God by His Spirit is the real author of the inspired Word...Is it not certain, then, as I have said, that these varying forms, so peculiar and striking, hide some spiritual mystery? And would it not have been more respectful to the Word if the translators of the common version had rendered these expressions literally, even though they did not know what they meant, rather than to obscure the sense altogether with capricious renderings?...They have rendered its various combinations in thirteen ways, viz.; age, course, world, eternal, since the world began, from the beginning of the world, ever, for ever, forever and ever, for evermore, while the world standeth, world without end, and, with a negative, never. These are not translations but paraphrases, and look to me like "handling the Word of God deceitfully," albeit it may have been unintentional...

The word rendered eternal or everlasting,...derived from aeon, is aeonios. It is very important to understand the meaning of the word, for as it is commonly understood, it is the main pillar of the orthodox doctrine of endless torment. That tremendous dogma stands or falls according to the meaning put upon this word...

We will endeavor to determine the meaning of this word aeonios, according to its origin, and also according to the sense of the passages where it occurs. The word...is an adjective derived from the noun, age, just as we form the adjective hourly from the noun hour, or yearly from the word year, or eternal for eternity. I have already explained aeon, whence the meaning of this derivative may be gathered. A derivative word cannot properly mean any more than the word from which it is derived. If aeon means eternity, then aeonios might mean eternal and not otherwise, but we have seen that aeon as used in the Bible does not and cannot mean eternity (the strongest upholders of the doctrine of endless woe make no claim that aeon means eternity); hence aeonios does not mean eternal...

The ages are periods of time during which God is working out His great plan of creating man in His own image. The ages are God's *times* (Acts 3:21, 1 Tim. 6:15, Eph. 1:10) during which he does His work (see John 5:17, Eph. 2:10, Ps. 74:12); hence God is called the God of the ages, the King of the ages, or the aeonial God. (1 Tim. 1:17 N.V. margin, Rev. 15:3 N.V.). The adjective aeonial has no more reference to duration, either long or short, than it has to color. It denotes a quality, a characteristic, not a quantity. It is not a time-word like eternal, annual, daily, etc., but a descriptive word like autumnal, vernal, or dispensational. God is absolutely eternal. From everlasting to everlasting He is God, but this is not the meaning of the word aeonial. This is not a word expressing God's duration, but simply expressing a characteristic of Him...

Matt. 25:46 reads, "These shall go away into aeonial punishment, but the righteous into life aeonial." It is argued that *aeonial* life is *endless* life; hence *aeonial* punishment is *endless* punishment. It is further argued that, if the punishment is limited, the life must be limited, the duration of each being expressed by the same word, and thus a disbelief in an endless *hell* destroys the doctrine of an endless *heaven*. The two stand or fall together. All this seems very conclusive to the majority of Christians. In fact, it seems to them absolutely unanswerable, and hence they feel compelled to believe in an endless hell in order to preserve their belief in an endless heaven...

The word aeonial has the force of *belonging to* or *in connection with* the ages. Anything that is peculiar to these age times and stands in connection with them is said to be aeonial, as, for example, aeonial salvation, aeonial redemption, aeonial inheritance, aeonial fire, etc. (See Heb. 5:9, Heb. 9:12, Jude 7.)...

The whole difficulty with [Matt. 25:46] lies in the fact that Christians are ignorant of what *aeonial life* is. It is not mere endless existence. The adjective aeonial has no such meaning as endless; it *never* has that meaning in any scripture; it describes the *kind* of life, not its duration. Jesus gives us a definition of aeonial life in John 17:3; "*This* is life aeonial, *to know Thee,* the only true God, and Jesus Christ whom Thou hast sent." Does not this satisfy you? Christ's own words? As plain and direct as can be? Knowledge of God and of Christ is life aeonial; that is to say, the life of the ages, God's work-days, in its final result will be a universal knowledge of God. "All shall know him from the least to the greatest." It has not been so in past ages, to be sure, but it will be so as the ages roll on. The "age times" have scarcely begun; there are yet "ages of ages" in the future; and, as their cycles roll, God will come to be known more and more until "the knowledge of the Lord will cover the earth as the waters cover the sea." This is the life that shall yet characterize God's "age times"; *this* is life aeonial. I have no doubt but that life thus attained to in "the ages to come" by a re-created race will continue on and on forever, for we are to be like God, deathless, immortal, "neither can they die any more"; but this fact of the endlessness of that life is not implied in the word aeonial, but is plainly taught in other scripture. Aeonial describes the *kind* of life as explained above. Even those who hold the orthodox view must admit that aeonial life is something more than mere endless existence. They believe that the damned in hell have that. Aeonial life, they must think, is an endless life of a certain kind—of bliss and enjoyment and perfect happiness—and this is true; but they fail to understand wherein the happiness and enjoyment consists, viz.—in a perfect knowledge of God. The highest enjoyment of which we are capable comes from knowing God. Nothing else will give us true happiness; nothing else will give us peace. *This—this is life;* all else is death. This, and this alone is man's perfect heaven.

Having thus determined the nature of aeonial life, it is comparatively easy to understand what aeonial punishment is. Not endless punishment! Such an idea is senseless as well as unscriptural. The purpose of punishment is not only the protection of society and the restraint of the offender, but also for his *reformation*. This latter should be the *main* purpose of punishment. Any punishment that is not conducive to this end is wholly unjustifiable. It is simply an attempt to overcome one evil with a greater evil. Now to talk about *endless punishment* is nonsense as much as it would be to talk of endless correction or endless reforming. You might speak of endless torture or endless suffering, but *endless punishment* is not a proper collocation of terms at all. I will add that the original word here rendered punishment signifies a punishment for the correction and bettering of the individual; hence it could not be endless. We have seen the true meaning of aeonial. Apply that meaning here and we have the correct idea of the phrase. Aeonial life, we have seen, is that *kind* of life peculiar to God's age-times; so aeonial punishment or *correction* (which would be a perfectly correct translation) is that *kind* of punishment that God will make use of in future ages to *correct* mankind. As of aeonial life so of aeonial punishment. It is not a punishment of a given *duration*, but of a certain *kind*—of such as will in the end work the reformation of the offender...

The meaning of aeonial, then, is *belonging to, peculiar to,* or *characteristic of* the ages... It is certain that the word does not mean endless or eternal... It does not even mean age-lasting, although it is sometimes so rendered for want of a better English word whereby to express it. Strictly speaking, however, the word does not mean lasting throughout the age any more than it means lasting throughout eternity. As Canon Farrar has said, "Even if *aeon* always meant eternity, which is not the case either in classic or Hellenistic Greek, *aeonial* could still only mean *belonging to eternity*, not *lasting through it*. The word *by itself*, whether adjective or substantive, *never* means endless." As we have no single word in English that properly expresses its meaning, it seems to me best to incorporate the word right into the language just as we have baptism, hades, etc. The form then, aeonial, I think is best, used in the sense explained in the foregoing. [46]

---

[46] A.P. Adams, *The Best from A.P. Adams Vol. 2*, pp. 40-52, Treasures of Truth, P.O. Box 89, Plenty, Canada, SOL 2RO. Original 19th century publication information unknown.

142

THE HELL OF SCRIPTURE
VS.
THE HELL OF HUMAN TRADITION

George Hawtin

Emerging out of 1940s Pentecostalism, what came to be called the Latter Rain revival began in Saskatchewan, Canada in 1948, largely under the leadership of former Pentecostal Assembly pastor George Hawtin (1909-1994.) Though the ensuing Latter Rain movement—whose emphasis remained mostly Pentecostal in nature and which was largely incorporated into the broader Charismatic movement of the 1960s—did not specifically emphasize universal reconciliation, Hawtin himself devoted much of his later life to it. His teachings appeared between 1960 and 1983 in his magazine "The Page." These were later published in a series of booklets on latter rain and universal reconciliation topics. He called his booklets the "Treasures of Truth" series, and this became the name of the small publishing operation that printed and continues to distribute his works. Hawtin was also instrumental in the republication, through Treasures of Truth, of most of the 19th century works of A.P. Adams. About this additional facet of his work, Hawtin wrote, "For many years I have felt that the gems dug from the mine of eternal truth through the anointed ministry of A.P. Adams, who wrote from about 1885 to 1925, were far too rich to be allowed to be lost to the present generation. I consider it, therefore, to be profitable that I should take in hand the task of compiling some of these precious unfoldings of truth that thousands of others, who have never had opportunity to be edified by his works, may now be blessed by them."

The doctrine of eternal punishment is based on a literal interpretation of some of the metaphors of scripture (to the complete neglect of many other scriptures which I shall presently show). No doctrine has ever been propounded with more confidence and greater bitterness nor with a grossness and coarseness more hideous and repugnant, and, in the face of the love and kindness of God, more inconceivable and incredible.

One of the theologians of the Church of England (Jeremy Taylor) speaks of the fate of the wicked in the following terms: "In hell every sense and organ shall be assailed forever with its own appropriate and most exquisite sufferings. We are amazed at the inhumanity of Phalaris, who roasted men in his brazen bull, but *that was a joy in comparison with hell.*" And here is what the renowned evangelist, C. H. Spurgeon, said on the same subject. "There is real fire in hell. Thy body shall be suffused with agony; thy head tormented with racking pains; thine ears tortured with horrid sounds; thy pulse rattling with anguish; thy limbs crackling in the flame; every vein a pathway for the fire to tread; every nerve a string on which the devil shall forever play the diabolical tune of hell's unutterable lament."

Is it any wonder that in the face of such sadistic humbug there has been a wholesale manufacture of infidels? All these statements may be a show of oratorical eloquence, but they are nothing more. They hold no part of truth. They deny every attribute of God. They make wisdom foolishness, turn eternal love into exasperated hate, make omnipotence helplessness, and make the justice of God the grossest injustice in the universe... It is contrary to the nature of God. It is contrary to the love of God. It is contrary to the the power of God. It is contrary to the scriptures and it puts God in the ridiculous position of being the almighty King of kings and Lord of lords yet having in His dominion a pocket of hate and resistance that even He cannot overcome. Further than this it makes the mighty sacrifice of Christ that was made for all the world to be almost impotent in its power and scope. Worst of all it frustrates the purpose of God laid down in the beginning when He said, "Let Us make man in Our image and after Our likeness and let Us give him dominion."

Some will immediately ask me whether I do not believe in hell. My answer is very definite on this point. I most certainly *do believe* in hell, but the hell of the Bible and the hell of human tradition are not the same thing at all. The hell of tradition is *punitive*, hopeless, and eternal, while the hell of the scripture, like every judgment of God, is corrective, remedial, and restorative. I do not understand enough of this great truth to make broad claims about it, but I do want to say that the whole doctrine of eternal punishment stands on the shaky foundation of a misunderstanding of the Greek word aion. This word, which means age, has been translated into English in the New Testament by seven different English words. It is translated as age (twice), course (once), world (thirty-two times), eternal (twice). The adjective form of the word, aionios, appears as eternal (forty-two times), everlasting (twenty-five times), and forever (once). By translating the word *aion*, which means *age* and has a *time limit*, by such words as eternal, everlasting, and forever, etc., it is small wonder that confusion arises as to what the true meaning really is. I do not profess to be a student of either Hebrew or Greek, but any good Greek-English New Testament or any good concordance such as Young's or Strong's will give the exact meaning of all these words. If you will take time to study this thought through, you will find, as I have done, that there is not one instance in the New Testament where any condemnation is final, irrevocable, or unending. In such passages as this, "Depart from me, ye cursed, into everlasting fire," the true meaning is "Depart from me, ye cursed, into *age lasting fire*," which is a very different thing, for it shows that the condemnation is for a period of time and is *not* timeless. You have often heard people speak of the *unpardonable sin*, but, if you read it in the light I have mentioned, you will see that Jesus did not say it was unpardonable, but that it hath no forgiveness *unto the age.* The following is from the Emphatic Diaglott. "Indeed I say to you that all sins will be forgiven the sons of men and the blasphemies with which they may revile; but whoever may blaspheme against the Holy Spirit has *no forgiveness to the age*, but is exposed to *aionian* (age-lasting) *judgment.*" Mark 3:28, 29. The same is true in each case where the word occurs.

This truth may come as a shock to you as it did to me when I first discovered it. Indeed, you may reject it and continue on with the hopeless old traditions of unending torment, but all who cling to this pagan teaching...will be hard put to explain the scriptures which plainly declare that God has ordained a time for the restitution of all things. I have positively no hesitation in saying that I thoroughly believe that, as surely as everything began in God, everything will also *end in God,* for "from Him everything comes, by Him everything exists, and *in Him everything ends.*" Rom. 11:36 (Goodspeed and Moffatt). Nothing but this could satisfy almighty power, omniscient wisdom, eternal justice, and fathomless love. Any other teaching than this makes God to be the loser of His own plan, His own purpose, and His own creation. It makes Satan to be wiser and stronger than God while the Lord almighty, omnipresent, omniscient, has to content Himself with a tiny handful that He has plucked in desperation from the devouring fire that He had not anticipated...

The following scripture taken from Ephesians is one of the most *all-embracing* declarations to be found anywhere in the Bible. It plainly declares that *in the dispensation of the fullness of times* God is going to gather *all things in heaven and all things in earth into Christ.* I will quote it from two...different translators so that the full meaning may be impressed upon our minds.

"Having made known unto us the mystery of His will, according to His good pleasure which he hath purposed in Himself; that in the dispensation of the fullness of times He might gather together in one all things in Christ, both which are in heaven and which are on earth, even in Him." Eph. 1:9, 10. (Authorized)...

"It is in Him and through the shedding of His blood that we have our deliverance—the forgiveness of our offenses—so abundant was God's grace, the grace which He, the possessor of *all wisdom and understanding, lavished upon us,* when He made known to us the *secret of His will,* and this is in harmony with God's merciful purpose for the *government of the world when the time is ripe for it*—the purpose which He has cherished in His own mind of *restoring the whole creation* to find its one *head in Christ;* yes, *things in heaven and things in earth* to find their *one head in Him."* How I rejoice and how I exult in such a glorious hope of universal reconciliation! What a day it will be when the fires of God have devoured the adversary that has existed in every man, when every evil work has been burned up and every man presented purified and faultless before the throne of His glory with exceeding joy...

The truth of final and universal reconciliation...fills the theme of Scripture. Why do we pass so lightly over the great statements of Paul with reference to the fall and redemption of man? He points out continually that, as sin with all its dire results passed upon us all because of the disobedience of *one man,* so righteousness passes upon us all through the righteousness of *one man,* Jesus Christ. Notice the convincing terms used in Romans 5:15-21. "Adam prefigured Him who was to come, but the gift is very different from the trespass. For while the rest of men died by the trespass of one man, the grace of God and the free gift which comes by the grace of the one man, Jesus Christ, overflowed far more richly upon the rest of men. Nor is the free gift like the effect of one man's sin; for while the sentence ensuing on a single sin resulted in *doom, the free gift ensuing on many trespasses issues in acquittal.* For if the trespass of one man allowed death to reign through that one man, *much more* shall those who receive the overflowing grace and free gift of righteousness reign in life through one, through Jesus Christ. When then, as one man's trespass issued in doom for all, *so one man's act of redress issued in acquittal and life for all.* Just as one man's disobedience made all the rest sinners, *so one man's obedience will make all the rest righteous.* Law slipped in to aggravate the trespass; sin increased, but grace surpassed it far, so that while sin had reigned the reign of death, grace might also reign with a righteousness that ends in life eternal through Jesus Christ our Lord." (Moffatt).

It should not be necessary to enlarge on this all-inclusive statement. Nothing could be more reasonable and just than that which Paul has explained in the passage above—that since death passed upon *all men* because of Adam's disobedience, so life and righteousness will eventually pass upon *all men* because of Christ's obedience. For as by the disobedience of *one* many were made sinners, so by the obedience of *one* shall many be made righteous. The multitudes of earth who have never heard of Adam are none the less affected by his disobedience. It is equally true that those who have not heard of Christ are affected by His righteousness. Christ is the Saviour of *all men*, especially of those who have the privilege of hearing and believing, for they are able to partake of the benefits of His redemption here and now...

There are always those people who object to this truth on the grounds that the preaching of universal reconciliation will make Christians and unsaved careless. People who want to be careless will always find an excuse to be careless and they will have to suffer the result of their carelessness in the judgment. The knowledge of God's purpose does not make true men careless. It makes them long to become a part of His will and part of His eternal purpose. We can embrace every travail in understanding, grace and love, when we clearly see it is working for eternal good according to His purpose which He purposed in Christ before the ages began.

Some have declared that if they believed that all men would eventually be saved, they would just throw up everything and have a good time. Such people might well ask themselves for what purpose they are serving God now. If they are only serving God because they live in dread of eternal torment, then they are serving as slaves in fear of a tyrant, but those who see God's purpose serve God because they *love Him* and long to partake of His glorious plan...

God has planned to reconcile to Himself all things both in heaven and earth. Even at this very moment *the full price* of the reconciliation of the universe and everything in it has been paid. Dare any man say that this is not what Paul was teaching when he wrote this all-embracing truth, "And having made peace through the blood of His cross, by Him to *reconcile all things to Himself: by Him, I say,* whether they be things in earth or things in heaven. And you who were sometimes *alienated and enemies* in your mind by wicked works, yet *now has He reconciled* in the body of His flesh through death to present you *unblamable and unreprovable* in His sight." Col. 1:20-22. The reconciliation purchased by the precious lifeblood of the Son of God, even Jesus Christ our Lord, will be carried out in every remote corner of the universe until the vision of John will be complete as he said, "And every creature which is in heaven, and on the earth, and such as are in the sea, and all that are in them, heard I saying, Blessing, and honor, and glory, and power, be unto

Him that sitteth upon the throne, and unto the Lamb for ever and ever." [47]

---

[47] George Hawtin, *According to the Purpose,* pp. 21-29, 41, Treasures of Truth, P.O. Box 89, Plenty, Canada, SOL 2RO.

A GRADUALLY REVEALED PLAN

A.R. Symonds

The immense diversity of opinion among those who alike appeal to the Scriptures as the source of their beliefs is not, I think, without significance...Surely the very existence of such diversity is of itself an indication that the Bible is by no means as yet understood in all its completeness, that though it be a completed revelation its *meaning* is still far from being exhausted. If, then, it comes to pass that, from time to time, new truths are out of it brought to light, and that former inferences from it are corrected or modified, this is after all only what should have been anticipated.

For, as up to the close of the written Word it was the divine method to impart truth in successive and progressive portions, one portion not only supplementing but even sometimes correcting the notions gathered from a former, so seems to be the will and purpose of God, since those revelations were completed, that his Church should not all at once, but gradually and progressively, attain to the knowledge and understanding of what this written Word reveals. And, indeed, with this end in view, the Word of God seems to have been so framed as to be in some measure for a veil as for a revelation. It consists of a 'letter,' and of a 'spirit,' or an outer form and of an inner meaning...

What our Lord said more particularly of his parables holds good, more or less, of all Scripture, that it is plain only to them to whom it is *given* to know the mysteries of the kingdom of heaven. Until, in other words, 'the spirit of wisdom' is imparted, even the best of men often strangely misconceive God's Word; by hearing they hear but do not understand, and seeing they see and do not perceive. Until the time comes when it pleases God to give to his Church the needful illumination, what strange ignorance and misapprehension it manifests about what subsequently becomes so plain.

It was really revealed in the Old Testament that the Gentiles were to be fellow heirs with the Jews of Messiah's salvation, and yet the most pious and learned Jews could not and did not see it; nay, even inspired Apostles only gradually learnt it in its fullness. Though the truth was contained in the Old Testament, yet it was 'a mystery' not made known until it pleased God that his Church *should* understand it...

So has it been with other truths, that while they were in the Divine Word men saw them not till the time came for them to be discerned. In short, it is with the Church as it is with the individual believer, it does not all at once attain to maturity of knowledge in divine things, but has to grow therein, and to get from age to age additional discoveries of God's Truth.

...May it not be that the doctrine now in question is 'a mystery,' hidden for the present from the Christian Church, but in due time to be recognized by it, when it shall please God to open the eyes of his people to see it in his Word? That it is in the Word I am most fully assured, and I cannot but think that the time is not very far off when the Church shall come to see and to acknowledge it; and when, in the same spirit that the Apostles and brethren who were in Judaea, on being convinced of the calling of the Gentiles, glorified God, saying, 'Then to the Gentiles also hath God granted repentance unto life,' good men will lift up their hands in holy joy and surprise, at the discovery of a hope in regard to their fellow-men, so infinitely larger than it had before entered into their hearts to conceive or understand. [48]

[48] A.R. Symonds, *The Ultimate Reconciliation and Subjection of All Souls to God Under the Kingdom of Christ*, Hamilton, Adams, & Co., London, 1878, pp. 5-7.

CRUDE EVANGELISM

Andrew Jukes

Andrew Jukes (1815-1901) was an English theologian who began his professional career as a Church of England as a deacon and curate in Hull. Experiencing a deciced shift toward "Baptist" teaching, he underwent adult baptism in 1843. Leaving the Church of England, he joined the Plymouth Brethren, then later founded an independent chapel in Hull. He published his reasons for leaving the Church of England in a tract called The Way Which Some Call Heresy. As a believer in universal reconciliation, Jukes became one of its leading proponents in England. His landmark book, written in response to a friend who was struggling with the doctrine of everlasting punishment, originally entitled The Second Death and the Restitution of All Things, was published in 1867. Subsequently released under the second half of the title only, the book was widely read throughout the world at the time and resulted in Jukes being denounced as a heretic. The Restitution of All Things has been a stable classic of universal reconciliation studies ever since. It is one of the best-selling of all books written on the subject. Jukes' classics The Law of the Offerings and The Names of God have also mostly remained in print since Jukes' lifetime and have kept his name before the public eye.

Will Christ there [after death] be another Christ from what He was here? Can He there look on ruined souls without the will to save; or is it that in glory, though the will is there, the power to save is taken from Him?

And will the glory change His members too,—change them back to love their neighbor as themselves no longer? Shall a glimpse of Christ now make us long to live and die for others; and when, by seeing Him as He is, we are made like Him, shall our willingness to die and suffer for the lost be taken from us?

Will this be being made like Him? If what is so generally taught is the truth,—and I can scarcely write it,— Christ there will be unlike Christ here: He will, if not unwilling, be yet unable, to save to the uttermost. Nay more,—so we are taught,—instead of weeping over the lost, as He wept here, He will feel no pang, while myriads of His creatures, if not His children, are in endless torment. Then at least He will not be, 'Jesus Christ, the same yesterday, today, and forever.'

Is this blasphemy? Then who teaches it? Surely men cannot know what they are doing when they teach such doctrine. Do they not see how, because it is a lie, it hardens, and must harden, even converted souls who really believe it?

For if with Christ in heaven it will be right to look on the torments of the lost unmoved, and to rest in our own joy, and thank God that we are not as other men, the same conduct and spirit cannot be evil now...

Even true believers are injured more than they are aware, just in proportion as they really believe in never-ending torments. If not almost hopeless about the removal of any very subtle or persistent form of error, they show that they have very little faith in the power of unwearying love to overcome it. Why should they not allow some evil to remain if the Lord of all permits it for ever in His universe; or how should they expect to overcome evil with good, when, according to their creed, God Himself either cannot or will not do so through ages of ages? Why should they not therefore after a few brief efforts leave the willful and erring to their fate, since the God of patience Himself, according to their gospel, will leave souls unchanged, unsaved, and unforgiven forever?

With their views they can only judge the evil: they do not believe that it can be overcome by good, or that those now captive to it can and must be delivered by unfailing love and truth and patience. Even the very preaching of the gospel is affected by this view; for men are hurried by it into crude and hasty work with souls—unlike Him who 'stands at the door and knocks,'—by which they often prematurely excite and thus permanently injure the proper growth of that 'new man,' whom they desire to bring forth. Blessed be God, His grace is over all; and He is better than His most loving children think Him; and our mistakes about Him, though they hurt His people and the world, can never change His blessed purpose. [49]

---

[49] Andrew Jukes, *The Restitution of All Things,* Longmans, Green, & Co., London, pp. 156-8.

WHERE DOES RESPONSIBILITY LIE TO CURE SIN?

A.R. Symonds

Ponder the facts of the case. By no impulse of his own will, by no act of his own, each human being comes into existence...of endless duration. Over this existence he has no power, to shorten or terminate it...for what we call death does in no wise curtail *existence*.

Again, by no fault of his own, each human being brings with him into existence a nature predisposed to sin...tainted moral affections, a vitiated and perverted will. This depraved constitution he is born with, it is transmitted from father to son, being the fatal inheritance of the children of men, as descendants of their fallen ancestor, the first man....

As a natural and necessary consequence of their being so constituted and so circumstanced, misery in manifold forms attends the children of men; a misery that cannot but be perpetual unless the evil of their nature can be cured in its root and core....

But it is not in man to effect this cure. Left to himself he neither ever would nor could accomplish it. Therefore has it been divinely undertaken and provided for, by the introduction of that economy of grace which is called the kingdom of heaven...in all respects it is complete and adequate for the recovery of man from sin and ruin so...it contemplates nothing short of this—the reconciliation and subjection of all things to God.

Here, then, let us pause for a moment to consider the probabilities or the improbabilities of the case, as they arise out of the facts just stated.

Is it *a priori* probable, or rather do we not instinctively feel it to be most *improbable*, that born as human beings are into the world with a nature prone to evil, and throughout their life on earth subjected to constant and pressing temptation, countless millions of them should for a few years of sin be consigned by a God of infinite love and justice to never ending torment? The longest life is but a moment compared with eternity, yet for the sin of that brief space, there is a theology which bids us believe, everlasting perdition will be the doom. The idea conflicts violently with the most elementary, as with the profoundest notion, of divine justice and goodness.

Now, let it not be objected here that we are not competent to judge of those attributes, or to say that this or that is fitting or not fitting in regard to them. I answer that God himself recognizes our capacity to judge of them by appealing to our own sense of them, and bidding us to imitate them.

It is written, "Be ye holy, for I am holy." We are told to be perfect even as our Father in heaven is perfect. We are exhorted to be imitators of God as dear children. Human excellence, therefore, is but the reflection and copying of divine excellence.

This could not be, we could not be commanded to be like God, if moral attributes, as ascribed in supreme perfection to God, mean qualities altogether foreign to human conceptions of goodness, if they are not analogous *in principle* to what He has Himself defined and enjoined as goodness in his moral creatures. Rather may it be said that such is the link between the human and the divine, that then is man most human when he most approaches to the divine. That is human or inhuman which is in concord or conflict with those moral instincts which the Creator breathed into his creature, so creating him after his own image, and imparting to him of the divine nature. Impaired and dimmed as they may have been by the Fall, these moral instincts have never been obliterated. Even in the heathen mind they existed in such force and clearness as to constitute a criterion of judgment, and for an inspired apostle to appeal to. The very currency in all languages of such words as human and inhuman, kind and unkind, to denote feelings and acts suitable or unsuitable to man as man, is sufficient to attest the presence of those moral instincts in man as man.

It is as endowed with these instincts, emanations from Himself, and as capable therefore of appreciating divine excellence, that men are exhorted to imitate God. Human excellence cannot therefore differ from divine excellence in essence, but only in degree. What is abhorrent to our sense of the one, ought to be abhorrent to our sense of the other. And, indeed, we act upon this sense of what is fitting or not fitting to the divine nature when we repudiate thoughts, feelings, acts attributed by the heathen to God, and like St. Paul 'commend ourselves to their conscience,' by showing the incompatibility of such thoughts, feelings, and acts, with the goodness and justice of God.

And so, appealing to and acting on the same conscience, may that dogma be unhesitatingly pronounced *a priori* impossible...which attributes to God what universally would be stigmatized as harsh, cruel, and unjust in man. Therefore do we repudiate as *a priori* improbable, as intrinsically inadmissible, the dogma of endless torture as the punishment of sinners, because it ascribes to God what would be execrated in man.

For instance, were an earthly ruler to condemn the vilest criminal in his kingdom to be carefully kept alive in order that he might be subjected to perpetual torture, all humanity would shudder at it. Yet there is a theology which calmly attributes to the all just and loving God the determination to keep myriads of his subjects in never ending existence in order that they may undergo a never ending torment.

Were an earthly father to consign a child, however worthless, to unintermitted suffering, should we not say that those who offered their children to Moloch were saints in comparison? Yet we are asked by some theologians to believe that the heavenly Father will subject his disobedient children to torment without end and without remedy. Were any human legislature to ordain that all crime alike, great or small, of tender youth or hoary villain, of the tempted or the tempter, of the ignorant or the well instructed, whether once committed or oft repeated, that all crime equally should be liable to life-long torture...would not such a legislature be denounced as a monstrosity on earth?

Yet there is a theology that teaches that under the legislation of the All Wise and All Good everlasting torment will be alike the doom of the arch-rebel and his adherents, of the tempter and his victims; alike the penalty of the prolonged defiance of the one, extending through thousands of years, and of the brief disobedience of the other, brief, *i.e.,* in comparison, though it be the disobedience of the longest life allotted to man; alike the punishment of him who, created holy, with no inherent tendency of nature to evil, with no solicitation from it from without, yet became a rebel, and has ever since made it the one end of his existence to foment rebellion, and no less the punishment of those whose sin if that of the nature they were born with, a nature moreover incessantly exposed to temptation.

Does not that moral sense which God implanted in us,

as a witness for Himself, cry out at this as libel upon divine justice?

But to take a milder contrast. According to the theology we are now combating, both the hoary headed transgressor and the youthful transgressor, if they die impenitent, will alike perish everlastingly. For instance, a lad of wicked disposition and conduct dies at twelve years old, unconverted and impenitent. Now it will scarcely be alleged that *responsible* being commences at an earlier age than five or six. So then, for the sin of some six or seven years, this child, no less than a sinner of a hundred years, is to undergo an anguish, of modified intensity perhaps, but still unlimited in duration. Again, I say the moral sense revolts at this, as repugnant to the idea of divine equity. No just man, we instinctively feel, would so apportion punishment...to attribute it to God we feel is monstrous." [50]

[50] A. R. Symonds, *The Ultimate Reconciliation and Subjection Of All Souls To God Under the Kingdom Of Christ,* pp. 28-33.

TO WHAT LIMITS DOES GOD'S WILL EXTEND?

Andrew Jukes

Ought not the present to teach us something as to God's future ways, for is He not the same yesterday and today and forever?

We know that in inflicting present death His purpose is through death to destroy him that has the power of death, that is, the devil. How can we then conclude from this that in inflicting 'the second death' the unchanging God will act on a principle entirely different from that which now actuates Him? And why should it be thought a thing incredible that God should raise the dead who for their sin suffer the penalty of the second death? Does this death exceed the power of Christ to overcome it? Or shall the greater foe still triumph, while the less, the first death, is surely overcome?

Who has taught us thus to limit the meaning of the words, 'Death is swallowed up in victory'?

Is God's will to save all men limited to fourscore years, or changed by that event which we call death, but which we are distinctly told is His appointed means for our deliverance?

All analogy based on God's past ways leads to one answer. But when in addition to this we have the most distinct promise, that 'as in Adam all die so in Christ shall all be made alive,' that death shall be destroyed, that 'there shall be no more curse' but all things made new, and 'the restitution of all things'; when we are further told that 'Jesus Christ is the same,' that is, a Saviour, 'yesterday, today, and for the ages'; the veil must be thick, indeed, upon man's heart, if in spite of such statements 'the end of the Lord' is yet hidden from us.

To me, too, the precepts which God has given are in their way as strong a witness as His direct promises. Hear the law respecting bondsmen, and strangers, and debtors, and widows and orphans, and the punishment of the wicked, which may not exceed forty stripes, 'lest if it exceed, then thy brother should seem vile unto thee'; yea, even the law respecting 'asses fallen into a pit'; and hear the prophets exhorting to 'break every yoke,' to 'let the oppressed go free,' and to 'undo the heavy burdens'; hear the still clearer witness of the gospel, 'not to let the sun go down upon our wrath,' to 'forgive not until seven times, but until seventy times seven,' 'not to be overcome of evil, but to overcome evil with good'; to walk in love as Christ has loved us,' and to 'be imitators of God as dear children'; see the judgment of those which neglect the poor, and the naked, and the hungry, and the stranger, and the prisoner; and then say, Shall God do that which He abhors?

Shall He command that bondsmen and debtors be freed, and yet Himself keep those who are in worse bondage and under a greater debt in endless imprisonment?

Shall He bid us care for widows and orphans, and Himself forget this widowed nature, which has lost its Head and Lord and those poor orphan souls which cannot cry, Abba, Father?

Shall He limit punishment to forty stripes, "lest thy brother seem vile," and Himself inflict far more upon those who, though fallen, are still His children?

Is not Christ the faithful Israelite, who fulfills the law, and shall He break it in any one of these particulars?

Shall He say, 'Forgive till seventy times seven,' and Himself not forgive except in this short life?

Shall He command us 'to overcome evil with good,' and Himself, the Almighty, be overcome of evil?

Shall He judge those who leave the captives unvisited, and Himself leave captives in a worse prison forever unvisited?

Does He not again and again appeal to our own natural feelings of mercy, as witnessing 'how much more' we may expect a larger mercy from 'our Father which is in heaven'?

If it were otherwise, might not the adversary reproach and say, Thou that teachest and judgest another, teachest Thou not Thyself? Not thus will God be justified. But, blessed be his name, He shall in all be justified. And when in His day He opens 'the treasures of the hail,' and shows what sweet waters He can bring out of hard hailstones; when He unlocks 'the place where light now dwells' shut up, and reveals what light is hid in darkness and hardness, as we see in coal and flint, those silent witnesses of the dark hard hearts which God can turn to floods of light; when we have 'taken darkness to the bound thereof,' and have seen not only how 'the earth is full of God's riches,' but how He has 'laid up the depths in storehouses'; in that day when the mystery of God is finished, and He has 'destroyed all that which now corrupts the earth,'—then shall it be seen how truly God's judgments are love, and that 'in very faithfulness He hath afflicted us." [51]

---

[51] Andrew Jukes, *The Restitution Of All Things*, 1867, pp. 92-95.

ON COLOSSIANS 1:12-20

A.R. *Symonds*

And now, in winding up this discussion, I wish once more distinctly to place before the reader what it is that I have endeavoured to establish. My position is this, that the redemptive work and mediatorial reign of the Lord Jesus will eventuate in the ultimate reconciliation of all, in the final subjection and submission of all to God. Apart from the direct testimony of Holy Scripture to this effect, I contend that nothing less than this can legitimately be inferred from what we are told of the person and work of Christ, of the design of his incarnation, and of his investiture with universal power and dominion. Considering all these, it seems to me a necessary inference that the reign and rule of Him, to whom all things in heaven and earth have been made subject, must ultimately issue in the complete victory of divine grace and goodness over satanic might and malice.

It is not, however, a matter of inference only but of distinct and emphatic statement. Not to adduce again the several scriptural testimonies which have been already cited, let this passage, which has not as yet been advanced, be duly pondered.

"Giving thanks unto the Father, who hath made us meet to be partakers of the inheritance of the saints in light, who delivered us out of the power of darkness and translated us into the kingdom of the Son of His love; in whom we have our redemption, even the remission of our sins: who is the image of the invisible God, the First-born of all creation; for in Him were all things created, the things in the heavens and the things on the earth, things visible and things invisible, whether they be thrones or dominions, or principalities or powers; all things have been created by Him and for Him; and He is before all things and in Him all things subsist. And He is the Head of the body, the Church, who is the beginning, the First-born from the dead, that in all things He may be the first. Because it pleased the Father that in Him should all the fullness dwell, and through Him to reconcile all things to Himself, having made peace through the blood of his cross, through Him, I say, whether they be the things on earth or the things in the heavens."(Colossians 1:12-20.)

I am bold to ask, Can any statement be more clear and decided than that here made by St. Paul? He says that God was well pleased that in Christ should all the fullness dwell, the fullness, that is, of the Godhead, and through Him to reconcile all things to Himself, having made peace through the blood of His cross, through Him (he repeats) whether they be the things on the earth or the things in the heavens.

Is this the good pleasure of God, to reconcile all things to Himself through Christ, and can that good pleasure be frustrated or disappointed?

Were all things created in Christ and by Christ and for Christ, and did He, in and by and for whom they were called into existence, become man and suffer and die to win back and restore a fallen world, and shall the mighty purpose of His incarnation be in any wise thwarted, and His redemptive act fall short of His creative act?

Did the Son of God become a partaker of flesh and blood, that through death He might bring to nought him that hath the power of death, that is the devil, and after all shall the issue of the contrast between the Prince of Light and the Prince of Darkness be, what according to so-called orthodoxy it only will be that whereas Immanuel will save His thousands, Apollyon will slay his tens of thousands?

I cannot and do not think it.

Rather would I believe that sooner than that Satan shall snatch one trophy from the Lord of Hosts, he himself shall at last succumb, and laying down the weapons of his rebellion become himself a trophy of the might and the mercy of Him whom God highly exalted, and to whom He gave the name which is above every name, that in the name of Jesus every knee should bend of things in heaven and on earth and under the earth, and that every tongue should confess that Jesus Christ is Lord to the glory of God the Father. [52]

---

[52] A. R. Symonds, *The Ultimate Reconciliation and Subjection Of All Souls To God Under the Kingdom Of Christ*, 1878, pp. 225-228.

An Address to the Clergy

William Law

Priest, mystic, theologian, William Law (1686-1761) was a leading Christian and Enlightenment thinker and author whose extensive writings greatly influenced the evangelical movement of the 18th century and were read widely. Many are still considered devotional classics of Christendom, his most well-known title being A Serious Call To A Devout and Holy Life, published in 1728.

His mercy is indeed infinite, and His goodness above all conception... The Love that brought forth the existence of all things changes not through the fall of its creatures, but is continually at work to bring back all fallen nature and creature. All that passes for a time between God and His fallen creature is but one and the same thing, working for one and the same end, and though this is called 'wrath,' and that called 'punishment,' 'curse,' and 'death,' it is all from the beginning to the end nothing but the work of the first creating Love, and means nothing else, and does nothing else, but those works of purifying fire, which must and alone can burn away all that dark evil which separates the creature from its first-created union with God.

God's providence, from the fall to the restitution of all things, is doing the same thing as when He said to the dark chaos of fallen nature, 'Let there be light.' He still says, and will continue saying, the same thing, till there is no evil of darkness left in nature or creature. God creating, God illuminating, God sanctifying, God threatening and punishing, God forgiving and redeeming, are all but one and the same essential, immutable, never-ceasing working of the Divine Nature.

That in God, which illuminates and glorifies saints and angels in heaven, is that very same working of the Divine Nature, which wounds, pains, punishes, and purifies, sinners upon earth. And every number of destroyed sinners, whether thrown by Noah's flood or Sodom's brimstone into the terrible furnace of life insensible of anything but new forms of misery until the judgment day, must through the all-working, all-redeeming love of God, which never ceases, come at last to know that they had lost and have found again such a God of love as this.

And if long and long ages of fiery pain and tormenting darkness fall to the share of many or most of God's apostate creatures, they will last no longer than till the great fire of God has melted all arrogance into humility, and all that is self has died in the bloody sweat and all-saving cross of Christ, which will never give up its redeeming power till sin and sinners have no more a name among the creatures of God. And if long ages hereafter can only do that, for a soul departing this life under a load of sins, which days and nights might have done for a most hardened Pharaoh or a most wicked Nero whilst in the body, it is because, when flesh and blood are taken from it, the soul has only the strong apostate nature of fallen angels, which must have its place in that blackness of darkness of a fiery wrath that burns in them and in their kingdom. [53]

---

[53] William Law, *Address to the Clergy,* pp. 171-173; Quoted from Andrew Jukes' *Restitution of All things,* 1867, 164-6.

COMPLETE VICTORY OR DUALISM?

Thomas Allin

Irish born Thomas Allin (1838-1909), like many of early pioneers in universal reconciliation studies, lived and wrote during the turbulent, invigorating, and spiritually controversial second half of the nineteenth century. Like MacDonald and so many others, he studied and trained for the ministry, took orders in the Church of Ireland, and served in a succession of curacies in Ireland before moving to England at the age of 39. He was not only a theologian but a noted botanist whose studies of the flowering plants and ferns of County Cork in Ireland produced one of the early definitive volumes on the subject. Allin's interest in the historical development of the doctrine and denominational influences of universalism led to his writing of what has become one of the true classics of universal reconciliation studies. The book now known simply as Christ Triumphant was originally published in 1885 by T. Risher Unwin, as THE QUESTION OF QUESTIONS: IS CHRIST INDEED THE SAVIOUR OF THE WORLD? In 1888, Eliott Stock publishers of London, the publishers of George MacDonald's A Cabinet of Gems, released the book under the title, UNIVERSALISM ASSERTED: ON THE AUTHORITY OF REASON, THE FATHERS, AND HOLY SCRIPTURE. This later became CHRIST TRIUMPHANT: OR, THE LARGER HOPE ASSERTED ON THE AUTHORITY OF REASON, THE FATHERS, AND HOLY SCRIPTURE, or, as it is known today in the Concordant Publishing Concern edition, simply CHRIST TRIUMPHANT. One of my wife Judy's favorite Victorian authors, Edna Lyall, wrote an impassioned Preface to the 1890 edition of UNIVERSALISM ASSERTED.

CAN EVIL COEXIST ETERNALLY WITH PURITY?

The question of universalism is usually argued on a basis altogether misleading, *i.e.*, as though the point involved was chiefly, or wholly, man's endless suffering. Odious and repulsive to every moral instinct as is that dogma, it is not the turning point of this controversy.

The vital question is this, that the popular creed by teaching the perpetuity of evil, points to a victorious devil, and to sin as finally triumphant over God. It makes the corrupt, nay, the bestial in our fallen nature to be eternal. It represents what is foulest and most loathsome in man, *i.e.*, the most obstinate sin, as being as enduring as God Himself. It confers the dignity of immortal life on what is morally abominable. It teaches perpetual Anarchy, and a final Chaos. It enthrones Pandemonium as an eternal fact side by side with Paradise; and, gazing over its fetid and obscene abysses, is not afraid to call this the triumph of Jesus Christ, this the realisation of the promise that God shall be *"All in All."*

A homely illustration may make my meaning more clear. What should we say of a householder who, prizing purity before all things, and with ample power to gratify his tastes, should sweep into some corner every variety of abomination, there to rot on for ever under his sight?

Nor is this all, for it is precisely the least rotten, and offensive, of the mass of moral filth that he removes and cleanses, while permitting the foulest of all (*i.e.*, the most obstinate and the very worst sinners) to rot and putrefy for ever. Indeed, according to the current theology, it is exactly because the moral foulness of this mass is so great, that it must endure for ever.

I have spoken very plainly, for our opponents do not realise what it is they have been teaching, and still teach. I have spoken very plainly because of the moral scandal involved in lowering God below the level of humanity; because such teaching justly makes God odious to thousands; because of the manifold and painful evasions of the great moral issues involved;...because of scepticism justified and increased.

And how instructive is the evident perplexity our opponents feel in reconciling with the triumph of Christ the perpetual duration of that evil, which He expressly came to destroy (1 John 3:8)....

With all earnestness, I repeat that our choice lies between accepting the victory of Christ or of evil, and *between these alternatives only.*

Escape from this dilemma there is none. It avails nothing to diminish, as many now teach, the number of the lost; or to assert that they will be finally annihilated.

All such modifications leave quite *untouched* the central difficulty of the popular creed — the triumph of evil. Sin for ever present with its taint, even in a *single* instance, is sin triumphant. Sin, which God has been unable to remove (and has had no resource but to annihilate the sinner) is sin triumphant and death victorious.

THE FATAL LEGACY OF ROME

How strange, too, is the delusion, often advocated, viz., that all real objections to the traditional creed are met, if the grosser forms of teaching it are abandoned...do not shock the mass of men, do not mention a literal fire: that is to go too far; retain the agony, but be careful to apply the suffering to the highest part — to the spiritual nature...

Men's minds must be deeply drugged by prejudice, and the power of reasoning partly paralysed, when such pleas are advanced, or when they fancy that, by diminishing the area of damnation they elude all objections to endless evil. As though you could solve moral questions by process of arithmetic, or annul the devil's victory by diminishing the number of his victims. So long as one soul for whom Christ died remains in the devil's grip for ever, so long and so far, is the devil victor. Nothing can by a hair's breadth alter that fact....

Against this idea, which is working untold mischief, I earnestly protest. It is the fatal legacy, the *damnosa hereditas,* which the stern and narrowly legal mind of Rome, with a natural bent to cruelty, bequeathed to the Gospel.

The God, Who is Love, is thus in practice changed into an Almighty Proconsul, while the Saviour of Men is disguised in the garb of a Roman Governor. Not the mercy-seat, but the seat of judgment is presented to the eye. An inflexible code, and an unbending Judge rule all; on every side is diffused a sense of terror.

Love is subordinate, sin becomes the central fact; guilt, not grace, comes first.

"Our Father" to all practical purposes, disappears, while the great Taskmaster, or the Moral Governor, or the Accountant-General takes His place. It is not that in so many words the love of God and the divine Fatherhood, are denied, but that they are so often recognised in words only. Shrunken, atrophied, palsied, the doctrine remains, as in some country where the rightful monarch has not been formally dethroned, but has dwindled into a puppet.

Such a system may call itself the Gospel, may point to the support of the greatest names, and be taught in thousands of pulpits (often softened, but the same essentially), yet it is a counterfeit and no true Gospel.

Where has the bright and joyous Christianity vanished which covered the dark recesses of the Catacombs with every symbol, that could attest joy and triumph...?

...To these men the victory of Jesus Christ was a thing really believed in, a fact actually realised, and dominating all else. Because they believed that death, and its sting, was really, truly, universally *swallowed up in victory.* And so they loved to paint Christ radiant with youth and strength, true and absolute Conqueror of death and hell...Why is the Christ of religious Art now so sad, with anguished features and drooping head—is it because He mourns His approaching defeat?...Whither has gone the Vision so noble, so tender, and yet so strong, of the victorious Christ as He descends into Hades, and opening the prison doors brings the disobedient dead back to life?

Yes, "they have taken our Lord away and we know not where they have laid Him." They have taken "Our Father," too, "the All Father," and we know not where to find Him. For bread they give us a stony creed; judgment without mercy; hell without hope; evil without end; heaven without pity for the lost and suffering....

Whither, too, has vanished that happier and higher view of death, as a *cure*, as the remoulding by the Great Artist of His own Likeness and Image, a view so significant and taught by so many and so famous names? By what right have we virtually added to the Ancient Creeds the fatal clause, "I believe in an eternity of evil?"...Why has the important fact been steadily ignored, or even denied, of the wide diffusion of universalism in the primitive Church? Why has the Church delighted to accept a cruel and uncatholic Africanism from the Bishop of Hippo, while refusing the nobler and more catholic teaching which the Bishop of Nyssa and so many saints freely taught in the Church's greatest age?...

Augustianism has in fact leavened all Latin Christianity, banishing the nobler teachings of true catholicity. Thus, if God is to damn men eternally, there is a step certain to be taken..., vis, the degrading and slandering that nature which man has received from God, and which the Son of God assumed and wears for ever. Thus, too, the Incarnation loses its proper place; the true lesson of Creation is ignored; the fact of the divine Image and Likeness in every man is displaced and forgotten...

The Correct Alphabet Of the Gospel

We are forced to ask, Have these our teachers, learned aright the alphabet of the Gospel? If they had, could they talk as they do? For to say that God is "loving," is in fact to make love an attribute merely, like justice or wrath.

God is not loving, for GOD IS LOVE, a distinction which is vital; which affects the whole Christian scheme in its essence.

Nor is this error all. Our opponents seem not to understand what Love really is; else they could not accuse us of making light of retribution, because we insist that God is Love.

For the very essence of Love is misconceived, when it is confounded with mere good nature; forgetting the awful, inexorable, side of true (divine) love; forgetting, too, that this love is essentially inextinguishable.

With a gospel based on errors so cardinal...with the central fact wrong, what wonder if all the rest is out of gear? Who could expect astronomy to flourish, if men were taught that this earth is the centre, and not the sun?

So with the moral universe. If I place Sin at the centre, and not Love—I paralyse every motion, and wholly invert the divine order.

It is a sad fact, that...in so very few...Christian pulpits, is there preached a God, Who is even as good as an average parent. Those who so preach would themselves loathe the very touch of a human father or mother who should act, as they say God will act towards many...of His creatures...

But the question remains, and will remain until it receives due answer. Is God really Master? or is sin to oust Him from any part of His own house for ever?...

Again, I entreat my readers to pay no need to the delusive plea that claims victory for Christ, if He shuts up His enemies in hell...as though the perpetuation of evil in hell were not His defeat. But, in truth, the traditional creed is essentially, if not formally, dualistic. There is a Deity (nominally) supreme, and a rival demi-god, Satan. There are two confronting empires, destined to exactly the same duration. In the middle ages we find actually represented in a painting a rival Trinity, a Trinity of Evil...How profound is the revelation thus made of the beliefs ruling the minds of men, still   in those who believe that the devil is all but omnipotent, and practically omnipresent.

LET US GO TO THE BIBLE

Let us go to the Bible.

Those who have reason to shrink from this appeal are not the universalists, but are the advocates of endless sin; of a baffled Saviour; of a victorious devil. It is they who shut their eyes to the teaching of the Bible. It is they who make light of its repeated promises of a restitution of all things. It is they who make Scripture of none effect by their traditions.

To the Bible they come drugged by early prejudice; saturated with cruel traditions, to whose horror long familiarity has deadened the mind. And so it is, that many really cannot see the true force of Scripture, when it plainly asserts the restitution of all things.

Hence the painful evasions; the halting logic that honestly (for I gladly admit this) but blindly turns the Bible upside down, *i.e.,* teaching that all men drawn to Christ, means half-mankind drawn to the devil; all things reconciled through Christ means the final perdition of half the universe. The notion of the popular creed, *i.e.,* that God is in the Bible detailing the story of His own defeat, how sin has proved too strong for Him, this notion seems wholly unfounded.

Assuredly the Bible is not the story of sin, deepening into eternal ruin, of God's Son, worsted in His utmost effort; it is from the opening to the close the story of grace stronger than sin—of life victorious over every form of death—of God triumphing over evil.

A TRUER VIEW OF GOD'S HOLINESS

Once more I repeat that the larger hope *emphatically and fully accepts* the doctrine of retribution. Those who picture universalism as some easy-going system, which refuses to face the stern facts of sin and misery and retribution, are hopelessly wrong.

We press on all the impenitent the awful certainty of a wrath to come, and this with far more chance of acceptance, because taught in a form that does not wound the conscience; because we dare not teach that finite sin shall receive an infinite penalty.

Few things have so hindered the spread of the larger hope as the wholly and absolutely groundless notion, that it implies an inadequate sense of sin, and pictures God as a weakly indulgent Being, careless of holiness, provided the happiness of His creatures is secured.

In fact it is those who teach the popular creed, and not we, who make light of sin. To teach unending sin in hell, even in a solitary instance, and under any conceivable modification, is to teach the victory of evil. To us this seems at once a libel on God and an untruth—a libel because it imputes to God a final acquiescence in sin; an untruth, because it teaches that His Omnipotence breaks down at the very moment it is most needed, and that His Love and Purity can rest with absolute complacency, while pain and evil riot and rot for ever.

Here we may ask, can any light, however small, be thrown on this awful mystery of sin?...For all practical purposes, I reply, there are but two possible views of moral evil. It is endless as God Himself, which is in fact dualism; or it is temporary, and in God's mysterious plan, permitted only to serve a higher end...

I am not presumptuous enough to fancy that I have a novel solution to offer of this profound mystery, but if the Bible be truly from God, then no solution is possible which refuses...to treat seriously...[certain] striking passages, on the ground probably that reverence for the Bible is reverence for those parts of the Bible that suit our own views...

A Meeting Ground Between The Two Views

And this prepares us for a very interesting question, viz., whether the evil effects of long continued wilful sin ever wholly pass away.

It may be replied, perhaps never in some cases. Some men, if I may for the moment so apply our Lord's striking words, may, in some sense, enter into life halt and maimed. Obstinate persistency in sin may leave on the spirit a wound whose evil effects are permanent. There may be, for I will not attempt to decide, a permanent weakness, though the disease of sin be cured.

Two results of this deserve notice.

(I.) It furnishes us with a fresh answer to the plausible taunt cast at the larger hope as leading the careless to say, "if this be true I will have my fling, for all will 'come right at last.'"

On any view, your fling, I reply, will bring you "the wrath to come"—a retribution in proportion to the wilfulness of your sin. But, further, your fling *may* involve you in a penalty strictly everlasting. You may, though pardoned, for ever suffer from the numbness and spiritual weakness which your sin leaves behind.

(II.) May not this furnish a meeting place for reasonable men on both sides? For final and universal restoration is not opposed to perpetual penalty in a certain sense; because the wilful sinner, though saved, may yet suffer a perpetual loss...of the highest spiritual blessedness.

THE SELFISHNESS OF THE BLESSED

Further, every form of partial salvation is rooted in selfishness. This selfishness is largely unconscious, but not the less real. Most people will have noticed a shocking unwillingness, on the part of the so-called religious world, even to entertain the idea of universalism. The unspoken feeling is often this—"If hell is gone, perhaps my heaven is gone too."...

We have thus a heaven actually, in some true sense, built on hell; buttressed on endless misery and sin.

And this is received as the true Gospel of Jesus Christ. A degrading selfishness is popularised, nay, is sanctified; religion is tainted. Salvation becomes a sort of stampede for life...a chase, in which the Powers of evil are always catching the hindmost.

And most strange of all, this grotesque and tragic scene is gravely asserted to be the victory of Jesus Christ. I do not know whether all this is more strange, or more shocking. For what can be more shocking than that any of the Blessed should be for a moment happy in a heaven literally built over the anguish...of the lost—nay, so long as a solitary mourner sits for ever in hopeless despair....The Blessed are content to gaze placidly over the abyss of hell, their satisfaction unbroken; their joys undimmed, if not actually heightened, by the torments of the lost....And when, finally, the curtain falls on an universe darkened by endless sin, they actually call this the triumph of the Cross; and are content to retire into a heaven of ineffable selfishness, where love is paralysed, and the Spirit of Christ dead; not caring though the wail of the lost for ever rise; the husband grown for ever deaf to the agony of the wife; the mother unheeding the eternal agony of her child.

Dante inscribed over the gate of the mediaeval hell, "Abandon hope, ye who enter here." Our teachers bid us inscribe over the gate of heaven, words, if possible, more awful, "Abandon love and sympathy: abandon the spirit of Jesus Christ, ye who enter here."

They bid us sing—

"O saints of God, for ever blest,

In that dear home how sweet your rest."

How sweet your rest, O wives whose husbands for ever burn; O mothers, how sweet your rest, while your children for ever agonise. *In that dear home how sweet your rest!*

...these horrors are taught when...Agnosticism is so threatening; when Science looks on the Gospel with hardly disguised scorn. And too often, an ignorant, if well meaning, clergy are content to cry, "Have faith;" as though God were not the author of reason; as though loyalty to conscience were not the supreme duty of every rational being...

I am content at the bidding of faith to accept a mystery which transcends my reason; but to prostitute conscience, to dethrone the moral sense, is treason to God...

I do not mean wilful untruth, but I do mean that virtual falsehood stains almost the whole body of our religious literature.

Falsehood is to say one thing, while meaning another. Hence, to assert that the world is saved, while meaning that in fact half the world will be damned; that mankind is rescued, while meaning in fact that many...go to the devil forever: to do this in a thousand forms, in hymns, in sermons, tracts, treatises, is falsehood; and with such untruth our religious literature is, I repeat, *honey-combed through and through.*

THE INCONSISTENCY OF THE POPULAR CREED

So long as the popular creed and the Bible are held together, so long must this system of untruth continue.

We pray to "our Father," to Whom in the next breath we assign acts toward His own children more cruel than any to which the worst earthly parent would stoop. We thus degrade the Godhead below, far below, the level of humanity. What is left for us to worship, if the truth be a lie—if love essential be cruelty itself—if God be that, which I dare not write?

Nor is this all.

Having assigned to God acts of infinite cruelty, the popular creed goes on to assure us of His tenderness that *never* wearies—His love that *never* fails.

What falsehood, what cruel mockery is this, coming from those who really mean, that this unfailing, eternal Love watches to all eternity, callous and unsympathising, the undying evil, the endless agony of its own children.

A merchant who has two contradictory measures is dishonest; but what of the theologian, of whom the same is true, is he less dishonest?

It is cruel to torment a cat or a dog for five minutes, but to be callous to all eternity about the endless misery of a wife or a child, is quite right and good....

Let a criminal be tortured for an hour by human law, and all the civilised world is roused; but let the same criminal pass to torture without end, and these endless pangs do not disturb for a moment the raptures of the inhabitants of heaven...

The apologies offered for the traditional creed are truly worthy of it. Thus many shelter themselves under the phrase, "God will do His best for every man." I can only suppose such an apology meant, not as an argument, but as an ill-timed piece of pleasantry.

For what are the admitted facts? An Almighty Being, Who is, on any possible hypothesis, perfectly free to create or not, yet *forces on* myriads of hapless children of His own the fatal gift of existence, knowing that in fact this life of theirs will ripen into endless misery and woe.

To call this doing His *best* for them is an abuse of language—could He do worse for them?

Few things are more wonderful in this whole question than the reluctance so many feel, to follow out these unhesitating convictions to their *only possible* legitimate conclusion—the rejection of that dogma, which flatly contradicts them...

FINAL APPEAL

I have shewn...by abundant evidence, the wide currency, in the early ages, of the broadest universalism, a fact too little known and ignorantly denied. May I again point out that this universalism was essentially based on Scripture, and that it has been re-echoed in later years by the most saintly souls.

You may search in vain in all the annals of English religion for a name more saintly than W[illiam]. Law, the universalist.

Men talk of the "laxity" of universalism. Was it this "laxity" that recommended it to the glowing devotion of Law...to Origen, whose life was one continuous prayer; to a crowd of men like-minded in the early Church? Was the devout Erskine of Linlathen drawn by this "laxity" to universalism, or Charles George Gorden, or Florence Nightingale? ...Or was it not that these, like so many of the early saints, had caught more truly the Spirit of Him, the All-Father, Who loving, loves to the end, Who seeks the lost, till He finds them?...

To attempt to introduce fresh ideas, especially in things religious, into minds saturated with doctrines taught in childhood, and hallowed by so many ties, has been well compared to trying to write on paper already scribbled over...

I have steadily sought in these pages, even when necessarily most outspoken, to recognise the perfect sincerity of my opponents; my quarrel, when most earnest, is not with individuals, but with a system. Here I would make a final appeal and ask, if some who read will not try to rise to higher levels, and to see in the larger hope the only view worthy of the All-Father, and of His Justice, which is the handmaid of His Love.

Alone this hope explains the wonders of our creation in God's Image; alone it satisfies the majesty of Love and its unquenchable thirst to raise the fallen, and most of all to save finally the most hopeless, the most unrepentant. Alone it really teaches that with God "All things are possible:" alone it sweetens every sorrow, and wipes away every tear.

By its light alone we are able to gaze at the very saddest depths of sin, and in its worst discords to hear an undertone of hope.

It alone enables us to believe truly in the Eternal Goodness, and its final victory: by it alone do we gain a full and adequate idea of the divine Unity...—One Will, One Love, One Law, One Lord, and "One far-off divine even to which the whole creation moves."...

Therefore in these pages I have pleaded for the larger hope. Therefore I believe in the vision, glorious, beyond all power of human thought fully to realise, of a "Paradise regained," of an universe from which every stain of sin shall have been swept away, in which every heart shall be full of blessedness in which "God shall be All and in All." — *Amen.* [54]

---

[54] Thomas Allin, *Christ Triumphant,* 1890, pp. 285-321.

Should We Keep Silent?

Andrew Jukes

Difficulty Of Complete Victory Being Received

Such then I believe is the testimony of Scripture as to the purpose and way of God our Saviour. That it will be judged as false doctrine by those, who, like Israel of old, can see no purpose of God beyond their own dispensation, is as certain as that Israel slew the prophets, and rejected the counsel of God toward sinners of the Gentiles; that it will be hateful also to fallen spirits may be seen from the way in which proud souls in every age rebel against the gospel. Their thought is that they shall continue for ever. Very humbling is it to think that all their pride and rebellion must be overthrown.

Even with true souls, who have been teaching another doctrine, there must be special difficulties in receiving a truth which proves them to have been in error. Now therefore, as of old, Samaritans know Christ as "Saviour of the world," while masters of Israel reject Him in this character.

For teachers to learn is to unlearn; and this is not easy. Nor can we expect that those, who occupy the chief seats in the synagogue, will readily descend from them and humble themselves, not only to take the place of learners, but to be reproached for doing so. How can masters of Israel eat their own words?

Even those who are willing to be taught are fearful. The consciousness that they are liable to err, and may be deceived, makes them cling to that which they are accustomed to. All these things, and still more our natural hard thoughts of God, are against the spread of the doctrine [of universal restitution].

But if it be God's purpose, it shall stand, and each succeeding age shall make it more manifest. God will at last surely cure all men of their mistrust of him...

SHOULD WE KEEP SILENT?

It is the lie, that He is a destroyer and does not love us, which has kept and yet keeps souls from Him. And though some argue that the doctrine of final restitution, even supposing it to be true, ought not to be whispered, except with great reserve, because men will abuse it, I cannot but think their prudence unwise, and that the truth, when God has revealed it, may be trusted to do its own work.

Of course this truth, like every other, may be abused. What good thing is there which may not be perverted?

The Bible and the gospel itself may be wrested to men's destruction, and Christ Himself be made a savour of death to those He died for. But surely this is no reason for locking up the Bible or the gospel, or for keeping back or denying any truth which God has graciously revealed to us.

And when I think of past objections to the gospel, that if grace is preached, men will abuse it and sin that grace may more abound,—when I remember how the doctrine of justification by faith has been opposed, on the ground that it must undermine all practical godliness,—when I see how God's election, clearly as it is revealed in Holy Scripture, is denied by some, who, wiser than God, think that such a doctrine must be perilous to man and opposed to God's love and truth,—I have less faith in the supposed consequences of any doctrine, assured, that, if only it be true, its truth must in the end justify it.

I rather believe that if the exactness of final retribution were understood, if men saw that so long as they continue in sin they must be under judgment, and that only by death to sin are they delivered, they could not pervert the gospel as they now do, nor abuse that preaching of the Cross which is indeed salvation...

The World Would Receive These Truths Gladly

I cannot but think that this doctrine of final restitution would meet much of the hopeless skepticism which is abroad, and which is certainly increased by this dogma of never-ending punishment.

Men turn from the gospel and from the Scriptures, not knowing what they contain, offended at the announcement, which shocks them, that God who is love consigns all but a 'little flock,' the 'few who find the narrow way,' to endless misery. Even true believers groan under the burden which this doctrine, as it is commonly received, must lay on all thoughtful and unselfish minds...

Even more affecting are the words of Albert Barnes, as a witness to the darkness of the ordinary orthodox theology:—'These and a hundred difficulties meet the mind, when we think on this great subject; and they meet us when we endeavor to urge our fellow sinners to be reconciled to God, and to put confidence in Him. I confess for one that I feel these, and feel them more sensibly and powerfully the more I look at them, and the longer I live. I do not know that I have a ray of light on this subject, which I had not when the subject first flashed across my soul. I have read to some extent what wise and good men have written. I have looked at their theories and explanations. I have endeavoured to weigh their arguments, for my whole soul pants for light and relief on these questions. But I get neither; and in the distress and anguish of my own spirit, I confess that I see no light whatever. I see not one ray to disclose to me the reason why sin came into the world, why the earth is strewed with the dying and the dead, and why man must suffer to all eternity.' (*Practical Sermons*, p. 123)

Such confessions are surely sad enough; but they do not and cannot express one thousandth part of the horror which the idea of never-ending misery should produce in every loving heart. As Archer Butler says, 'Were it possible for man's imagination to conceive the horrors of such a doom as this, all reasoning about it would be at an end; it would scorch and wither all the powers of human thought.' [*Sermons, Second Series*, p. 333.—151-53]

WE BECOME AS WHAT WE WORSHIP

Can such a doctrine be true? If it be, let men declare it always and in every place. But if it be simply the result of a misconception of God's Word, it is high time that the Church awake to truer readings of it.

It is not for me to judge God's saints who have gone before. Their judgment is with the Lord, and their work with their God. But when I think of the words, not of the carnal and profane, but even of some of God's dear children...when I find Augustine saying, that 'though infants departing from the body without baptism will be in the mildest damnation of all, yet he greatly deceives and is deceived who preaches that they will not be in damnation' (*De peccatorum meritis*, lib. i cap. 16, 21) meaning thereby unending punishment; or Thomas Aquinas, that 'the bliss of the saved may please them more, and they may render more abundant thanks to God for it, that they are permitted to gaze on the punishment of the wicked;' (*Summa*, Part iii) or Peter Lombard, that 'the elect, while they see the unspeakable sufferings of the ungodly, shall not be affected with grief, but rather satiated with joy at the sight, and give thanks to God for their own salvation;' (*Sentent.* lib. iv) or Luther, that 'it is the highest degree of faith to believe that God is merciful, who saves so few and damns so many; to believe Him just, who of His own will makes us necessarily damnable;' (*De servo arbitrio*, 23, 1557)—when I remember that such men have said such things, and that words like these have been approved by Christians, I can only fall down and pray that such a night may not return, and where it yet weighs on men's hearts the Lord may scatter it.

For it is not unbelievers only that are hurt by such teaching. Those who believe it are even more injured. For our views of God re-act upon ourselves.

By an eternal law, we must more or less be changed into the likeness of the God we worship. If we think him hard, we become hard. If we think Him careless of men's bodies and souls, we shall be careless also. If we think Him love, we shall reflect something of His loving-kindness.

God therefore gave us His image in His Only-Begotten Son, that 'we with open face might be changed into the same image.' What that image was the Gospels tell. In word and deed they show that "God is love;" "bearing all things, believing all things, hoping all things, enduring all things; never failing,"...

Oh blessed gospel...Our unlikeness to Him proves how little we have seen Him; for 'we shall be like Him when we see Him as He is.'

WHAT SAITH THE SCRIPTURE?

I conclude as I began. The question is, what saith the Scripture?

If these hard views of God, which so many accept, are indeed the truth, let men not only believe them, but proclaim them ceaselessly.

If they are, as I believe, only misconceptions of the truth, idols of man's mind, as false and contrary to the revelation God has made of Himself in Christ as the idols of stone and wood and gold and silver were to the law of Moses, may the Spirit of our God utterly destroy them everywhere, and change our darkness into perfect day.

No question can be of greater moment, nor can any theology which blinks the question meet the cravings which are abroad, and which I cannot but believe are the work of God's Spirit. The question is in fact, whether God is for us or against us; and whether, being for us, He is stronger than our enemies. To this question I have given what I believe is God's answer.

And my conviction is that the special opening of this truth, as it is now being opened by God Himself, everywhere, is an evident sign and witness of the passing away of present things, and of the very near and imminent judgment of apostate Christendom.

A time of trial and conflict plainly is coming, between a godless spiritualism on the one hand, and on the other a so-called faith, which has lost all real experience...whose professors therefore have nothing to fall back on but a letter or tradition, which, however true, will in carnal hands be a poor defence against a host of lying spirits.

Alas for those who in such a trial, while calling themselves the Lord's, know nothing of hearing His inward voice or of being taught by His Spirit. But He yet says, 'He that hath an ear, let him hear what the Spirit saith.'

His grace, if sought, is still sufficient for us. May He more fully guide us into His own truth, and as a means open to us yet more His Holy Scriptures, which, like the world around, contain unknown and undiscovered treasures, even the unsearchable riches of Christ, which are laid up for lost creatures. [55]

---

[55] Andrew Jukes, *Restitution Of All Things*, Longmans, Green, & Co, London, 1867, pp. 149-60.

BIBLIOGRAPHY AND RECOMMENDED SOURCES

—A.P. Adams, *The Best From A.P. Adams,* Treasures of Truth, P.O. Box 89, Plenty, Canada, SOL 2RO. Original 19th century publication information unknown.

—Thomas Allin, *Christ Triumphant,* 1885, 1888—Concordant Publishing Concern, 15570 West Knochaven Road, Canyon Country, CA 91351.

—William Barclay, *A Spiritual Autobiography,* Wm. B. Eerdmans, Grand Rapids, MI, 1975.

—G.R. Hawtin, Treasures of Truth, P.O. Box 89, Plenty, Canada, SOL 2RO.

—Dr. Loyal F. Hurley, *The Outcome of Infinite Grace,* original date and publisher unknown.

—Dr. Jack Jacobsen, *Our Church Fathers Testify,* Redeeming Love Publications, 606 East Maryland Ave., St. Paul, Minn. 55101.

—Andrew Jukes, *The Restitution Of All Things,* Longmans, Green, & Co., London, 1867.

—A. E. Knoch, *The Mystery of the Gospel,* Concordant Publishing Concern. Bible scholar and translator A.E. Knoch wrote a number of books and pamphlets and founded Concordant Publishing Concern at the opening of the twentieth century. Concordane continues to make many materials available on universal reconciliation. Concordant Publishing Concern, 15570 West Knochaven Road, Canyon Country, CA 91351.

—A.E. Knoch, *All In All,* 1978, Concordant Publishing Concern, 15570 West Knochaven Road, Canyon Country, CA 91351.

—Adlai Loudy, *God's Eonian Purpose,* 1929, Concordant Publishing Concern, 15570 West Knochaven Road, Canyon Country, CA 91351.

—George MacDonald, *Unspoken Sermons, First Series,* Sunrise Books, P.O. Box 7003, Eureka, CA. 95502.

—George MacDonald, *Unspoken Sermons, Third Series,* Sunrise Books, P.O. Box 7003, Eureka, CA. 95502.

—George MacDonald, *Discovering the Character of God,* Bethany House Publishers, 11400 Hampshire Ave., S., Minneapolis, Minn. 55438.

—F.D. Maurice, *Theological Essays,* Macmillan & Co, 1853.

—Michael Phillips, *George MacDonald, and the Late Great Hell Debate,* Yellowood House, an imprint of Sunrise Books, 2013.

—Michael Phillips, *George MacDonald, Scotland's Beloved Storyteller,* Bethany House Publishers, 1987.

—Michael Phillips, *Hell and Beyond,* Yellowood House, an imprint of Sunrise Books, 2013.

—Rev. A.R. Symonds, *The Ultimate Reconciliation and Subjection Of All Souls To God Under the Kingdom Of Christ,* Hamilton, Adams, & Co., London, 1878.

LEBEN—*A periodical dedicated to the spiritual vision of Michael Phillips and the legacy of George MacDonald.*

LEBEN ISSUES 9-12—Articles on "George MacDonald and Universal Reconciliation."

The books of Michael Phillips and George MacDonald, as well as issues of *Leben*, are available through "The Bookstore" @ FatherOfTheInklings.com.